C000016065

Dissertation Writing in Practice

Hong Kong University Press thanks Xu Bing for writing the Press's name in his Square Word Calligraphy for the covers of its books. For further information, see p. iv.

Dissertation Writing in Practice
Turning Ideas into Text

Linda Cooley and Jo Lewkowicz

香港大學出版社
HONG KONG UNIVERSITY PRESS

Hong Kong University Press
14/F Hing Wai Centre
7 Tin Wan Praya Road
Aberdeen
Hong Kong

© Hong Kong University Press 2003

First published 2003
Reprinted 2004, 2006

ISBN 962 209 647 6

All rights reserved. No portion of this publication may be reproduced
or transmitted in any form or by any means, electronic or mechanical,
including photocopy, recording, or any information storage or retrieval
system, without prior permission in writing from the publisher.

British Library Cataloguing-in-Publication Data
A catalogue record for this book is available from the British Library.

secure on-line ordering
http://www.hkupress.org

Printed and bound by Nordica Printing Co., Ltd., Hong Kong, China.

Hong Kong University Press is honoured that Xu Bing, whose
art explores the complex themes of language across cultures,
has written the Press's name in his Square Word Calligraphy.
This signals our commitment to cross-cultural thinking and the
distinctive nature of our English-language books published in
China.

"At first glance, Square Word Calligraphy appears to be
nothing more unusual than Chinese characters, but in fact it is
a new way of rendering English words in the format of a square
so they resemble Chinese characters. Chinese viewers expect to
be able to read Square Word Calligraphy but cannot. Western
viewers, however are surprised to find they can read it. Delight
erupts when meaning is unexpectedly revealed."

— Britta Erickson, *The Art of Xu Bing*

Contents

Introduction

Recent years have seen a dramatic increase in the number of students registering for postgraduate studies. In particular many EFL/ESL (English as a Foreign Language/ English as a Second Language) students are choosing to carry out their studies in universities in English-speaking countries, such as Australia, the UK and the US, or in countries using English as the medium of instruction for university studies, where they will be expected to complete the writing of their dissertation in English. This has led to a growing body of research interest in the area of postgraduate dissertation writing in general, and in the difficulties faced by EFL/ESL postgraduates in particular. This interest has been occasioned by the acknowledgement in the academic community that there is no justification for believing that expertise in a specific discipline automatically ensures that a student will be able to communicate his/ her knowledge clearly in writing. Students, after all, engage in postgraduate studies because they are interested in conducting research, not because they are interested in writing *per se*. Indeed, many postgraduate students are relatively inexperienced writers. This is particularly the case for those students from disciplines where extended essays at undergraduate level are not the norm, e.g. many departments in the science and engineering faculties. Their lack of experience in writing leaves many postgraduate students in a state of bewilderment, bursting with ideas that they cannot easily communicate on paper and in need of practical help. It is for these students that our book is written, hence our title — *Dissertation Writing in Practice: Turning Ideas into Text*.

We should explain here that we use the term 'dissertation' throughout this book mostly in the interests of readability, as encountering 'dissertation/thesis' repeatedly may become rather tedious for the reader! We could find no satisfactory explanation for the difference between the two terms as both are used widely, and apparently interchangeably, in the literature; indeed, the dictionary defines one in terms of the other. In some countries there appears to be a preference for using 'thesis' at masters level and 'dissertation' at doctoral level, but in other countries the reverse is true. In our case, we have chosen 'dissertation', idiosyncratically maybe, out of a preference for the meaning of the Latin root of the word, *disserere* (to discuss) from *dis* + *serere*(to connect), as this is precisely what we would like students to do when using this book: discuss and connect.

This book is designed primarily, but not exclusively, for EFL/ESL postgraduate students who are preparing to write a dissertation in English. However, in our experience native speaker postgraduates can also benefit from many parts of the book, as it raises consciousness of issues related to academic writing at dissertation level that many native speakers are unaware of. The book concentrates on the writing of a dissertation, as opposed to an essay or term paper, and, as such, may not be so useful for undergraduates, although those undergraduate students who need to prepare a dissertation in their final year could find the book useful.

The book should also prove useful to scholars and researchers, both native and non-native speakers, who are preparing articles for publication in journals. Many of the language features focussed on apply equally to the writing of a dissertation and the writing of a journal article and, indeed, many of the examples we discuss are taken from journal articles rather than dissertations, as extracts from the latter are generally rather too lengthy to be included in a textbook. Throughout the book we attempt to draw the students' attention to the parallels and differences between the two genres to make the book useful for writers in both areas.

This book is founded on extensive research into the writing difficulties and needs of postgraduate research students at the University of Hong Kong. In the university approximately 90 percent of postgraduate students are expected to produce their dissertation in English although this is not their first language and, indeed, an increasing percentage of these students have not completed their first degree through the medium of English. The original research led to the development of courses in dissertation writing, which were so well received that they have now become compulsory for students registering in the Graduate School. This textbook has evolved from the materials developed for use on these courses. We believe the success of the course we teach is due partly to the fact that the materials have been designed to address problems with the writing of the dissertation, rather than research problems, and partly to the fact that the problems addressed are of a more complex nature than the sentence-level and paragraph-level difficulties that are more usually dealt with in books on academic writing.

The main objective of this book is to raise students' awareness of the linguistic characteristics of a postgraduate dissertation. The book focuses on the areas which students find difficult or different from other forms of writing they have been exposed to in their undergraduate studies. Its most distinctive characteristic is that it deals primarily with the linguistic features of extended pieces of writing, placing great emphasis on the writer's responsibility for the readability of the text. Each of the features introduced is illustrated through examples taken from actual writing at a level appropriate for the student. In addition, each chapter includes numerous tasks and exercises for the students to apply the concepts introduced to other extracts. Every chapter has a short section on the differences and similarities between dissertations and journal articles with respect to the feature focussed on in that chapter. Each chapter ends with a summary of the main points and further advice to students on what to look for when examining dissertations and articles in their own discipline.

As the book is based on several years' experience in teaching dissertation writing across a wide range of disciplines, it thus adopts a multi-disciplinary approach, taking examples from a wide selection of fields and encouraging discussion across the academic community. This has been done for a number of reasons. Firstly, it allows the book to be used by multi-disciplinary classes without any group of students feeling that they are not being catered for. This was considered to be an important characteristic of the book as it is generally not feasible within a university to run separate writing classes for different disciplines. Secondly, the use of reading materials from disciplines with which they are unfamiliar encourages students to concentrate on the language points that are being studied rather than the content of the extracts. Finally, this approach enables students to see that dissertation writers share common problems and that they can help each other to overcome these problems, even though they may not be researching in the same area. This is not to say that differences between disciplines are not acknowledged. Throughout the book, students are encouraged to examine texts written in their own fields to see where the language used diverges from the examples given.

ORGANISATION OF THE BOOK

The book is organised thematically according to the steps dissertation writers need to take when undertaking research and reporting on it. It focuses on the language used to achieve each step successfully. For example, the first chapter addresses the issue of 'Identifying the Research Gap'— the first step the writer has to take. It explains how the Introduction and the Literature Review share the function of creating a research space and looks at the language used for introducing one's own research and the way in which previous research is reported and used to create a research space justifying the need for the present research. The book covers all the major sections of a dissertation, i.e. the introduction, literature review, method, results, discussion and conclusion, but these sections are not necessarily the focus of the chapters. This is because much of the advice given throughout the book pertains to more than one given section and we believe it is important that students appreciate this. The book stresses that there are different ways in which a dissertation can be organised, other than the traditional manner of Introduction, Literature Review, Method, Results, Discussion and Conclusion. But it tries to point out that, despite differences in organisation, there are certain functions which are common to all dissertations and certain language that has to be used to carry out these functions.

HOW TO USE THE BOOK

This book is primarily intended to be used as a textbook by students attending courses on how to write a dissertation in English. Each chapter is organised to allow for several teacher-input sessions of both rhetorical and language features and each session is followed by group discussions/ personal study of examples and tasks to practise the language features of the points raised. However, the book should also prove useful for students studying on their own. There is an extensive Answer Key at the end of the book providing explanations for the responses to the tasks in each chapter. There are no lengthy writing assignments, as this book focuses on raising students' consciousness of features of dissertation writing that they are often unaware of, rather than providing writing practice. However, each chapter ends with suggestions for follow-up tasks; these tasks involve writing short texts to practise the features that have been covered in that chapter or analysing texts to see how the features are applied in the student's own field.

We hope that the book will prove valuable to those students faced with the daunting task of producing a dissertation and will make their academic path a little easier to tread.

ACKNOWLEDGEMENTS

This book is the result of courses that we have run for several years for postgraduate students at the University of Hong Kong. We would like to thank the many students on these courses, whose ideas have led to modifications of our original materials, and colleagues for their advice. Their input and suggestions have been invaluable to the development of this book. Thanks are also due to all those students who have given us permission to use extracts from their assignments and dissertations.

The texts utilised as examples and tasks throughout the book are acknowledged in the Sources section at the end. Where no acknowledgement is listed, that text is either the authors' own work or from the draft of a student's work. Slight modifications have been made to student texts where the original contained a language error, e.g. a mistake in spelling or verb tense, in order not to present erroneous examples of language use to readers.

1 Identifying the Research Gap

When you come to write your dissertation, you need to convey three types of information to your readers: you have to explain the background which led to your study; you must describe how the study was carried out and finally you discuss your findings and present the conclusions that you have reached. This first chapter considers how a writer presents the background information, that is, the introductory part of a dissertation. (As we explained in the Introduction, throughout this book we are using the term 'dissertation' to apply to what is variously called a dissertation or a thesis.)

Before we do this, however, we should take a look at what research itself is. Research is defined by *Collins Cobuild English Language Dictionary* (third edition, 1991) in the following way:

> Research is a detailed study of a subject or an aspect of a subject. When you do research, you collect and analyse facts and information and try to gain new knowledge or new understanding.

As we can see from this definition, a researcher is trying to find *new* knowledge or *new* understanding. For any research to have a purpose then, there must be some gap in the current knowledge. The gap may be in the form of a newly discovered problem or an incomplete answer to a previously researched problem. It may be that a phenomenon has not been investigated in a particular place before or with a particular group of people or from a particular perspective. Whatever the situation, the first task a writer faces is how to make this gap clear to readers. This is done by explaining what stimulated the study and by reviewing the relevant literature to show what was known and what was not known at the outset of the research.

There are several ways of organising this introductory material in a dissertation. The first chapter may consist of a short introductory section of just two or three paragraphs, followed by a detailed analysis of the literature in the field. (We will call this a Type 1 dissertation.) Alternatively, the introductory chapter can be extended to form a chapter on its own, before the literature is reviewed in detail in a second chapter (Type 2 dissertation). These two types of organisation are perhaps the most common ways of presenting the introductory material. However, in some dissertations, particularly in the humanities, there is no separate section or chapter called the Literature Review or Literature Survey, just as there are no Method and Discussion chapters. These are topic-based or text analysis dissertations (Type 3). After an introductory chapter, which explains the overall theme of the research, each individual chapter of the dissertation consists of its own introduction and an analysis of text or discussion of the topic of that chapter, with reference throughout to the literature. Yet one more type of dissertation, though a less common type, is a dissertation which consists of a compilation of published research articles (Type 4). The introductory chapter here is similar to that of a Type 3 dissertation in that its function is to explain what links together all the separate studies reported in the articles which form the chapters. (You can see a detailed breakdown of different types of dissertation organisation in Chapter 5.) In the following sections, for ease of reference, we will use the term Introduction to refer to both the introductory section of a Type 1 dissertation and the introductory chapter of Types 2, 3 and 4 dissertations.

WRITING AN INTRODUCTION: MAIN STEPS

The overall purpose of an Introduction to a dissertation is to make the reason for the research clear to the reader. You could see the Introduction as starting the reader off on a journey through the dissertation. It has to give the reader some idea of the starting point of the journey, i.e. the situation which has led the writer to conduct his/her research in the first place, and then explain how the writer will travel to reach the chosen destination, that is, what the research will do to arrive at a new situation. Alternatively, you could see the Introduction as an explanation of how you will make changes to a building that is in need of renovation or extension: first of all you must describe the present building and point out its drawbacks before you explain what changes you propose to make to it.

However you picture the Introduction, it is clear that to achieve its overall purpose of explaining the reason for the research, this section/chapter has to identify the research gap that you intend to fill. To do this, there are generally four basic steps which the writer needs to take. These steps are presented in Table 1.1 below:

Table 1.1 Four basic steps to take in an Introduction

Step 1: Describe the problem/difficulty/situation that interests you.
Step 2: Establish, briefly, what has already been said and done in this area.
Step 3: Point out what has not been done/what is not yet known, i.e. the gap.
Step 4: Explain what you hope to do to add to the body of knowledge.

(Based on Swales' CARS [Creating a Research Space] model in Swales, J. (1981) *Aspects of Article Introductions*, University of Aston, Language Studies Unit)

If we look at the Introduction below taken from a journal article in the field of dentistry, it is easy to identify the four steps outlined in Table 1.1, even though we may not understand all the concepts presented:

EXAMPLE 1.1

[Square brackets have been added to indicate sentence numbers for ease of reference.]

DNA Ploidy and Proliferate Pattern in Benign Pleomorphic Adenomas of Major Salivary Glands

Pleomorphic adenoma is the most common salivary gland neoplasm and frequently recurs after simple surgical excision due to incomplete removal of its unencapsulated portion or to the presence of "satellite nodules" [several references given in the original]. [1] Malignant change of the lesion is known to occur, although its incidence is frequently difficult to estimate when based solely on qualitative histopathological features [several references given in the original]. [2] It is generally agreed that the vast majority of these neoplasms are essentially benign, but the existence of locally malignant variants, or lesions with malignant potential, has been described [several references given in the original]. [3] Further, it has been suggested that truly malignant [reference given in the original] or semimalignant [reference given in the original] variants exist. [4]

Flow cytometry (FC) has unique advantages for examining the DNA content of tumour cells and the technique has been used for diagnostic and prognostic assessment of a wide variety of tumours [several references given in the original]. [5] However, reports of the application of FCM to salivary gland tumours are few and the number of cases studied in each report have been very limited [reference given in the original]. [6] In the present study, we examined 10 pleomorphic adenomas from major salivary glands using FCM, with normal salivary glands and chronic sialadenitis lesion as control. [7] Our purpose was to examine the DNA content and proliferative patterns in the lesions in order to detect any possible correlations between FCM analysis, diagnosis and the biological behavior of these tumours. [8]

Steps	Sentence(s)
1. Describe the problem	1
2. Establish what is already known	2–5
3. Point out the gap	6
4. Explain how the gap will be filled	7 and 8

An analysis of this Introduction shows that what the writers are doing is establishing that there is a gap in the knowledge concerning a particularly common, and frequently recurring, cancerous growth in the salivary glands. They do this by first telling their readers what has already been established by previous researchers (Sentences 1–5); then, they proceed to point out the limitations of the previous studies

(Sentence 6) in order to justify their own study, which seeks to overcome the limitations and fill the gap in knowledge by using a technique that has rarely been used in this area of dental research (Sentences 7 and 8). They have, therefore, produced an Introduction which fulfils the requirement of identifying the research gap for the reader.

TASK 1.1

Look at the following Introduction from a journal of literary semantics and see if you think this also successfully identifies the research gap. Can you identify which sentences carry out the four different steps?

[Square brackets have been added to indicate sentence numbers for ease of reference.]

1. Introduction

Over the last couple of decades, the study of literary text worlds has made considerable advances under the influence of the possible-world frameworks originally developed within modal logic and logical semantics. [1] The notion of possible worlds, which was devised by philosophers and logicians to solve a number of logical problems, has been increasingly extended to provide a theoretical base for fundamental issues within the semantics of fictionality. [2] These include the logical properties of sentences of and about works of fiction, the ontological status of fictional entities, the definition of fiction, and the nature of the worlds projected by different types of fictional and/or literary text. [3] More specifically, possible-world models have been used in order to:

(a)   describe fictional worlds as complex modal structures made up of a central domain counting as actual and a number of secondary domains counting as non-actual (such as characters' belief worlds, wish worlds, fantasy worlds, etc.) (e.g. Eco 1979, 1990; Pavel 1986, Ryan 1991a);

(b)   classify text worlds on the basis of the accessibility relations (Kripke 1971) that link them to the actual world, i.e. on the basis of criteria such as logical possibility, physical possibility, and so on (e.g. Maitre 1983, Ryan 1991a). [4]

The vast majority of possible-world approaches to the study of fiction have focused on literary narratives (e.g. Dolezel 1976a, 1976b; Maitre 1983, Ryan 1991a), with the occasional reference to drama (e.g. Pavel 1986). [5] Poetry, on the other hand, has been largely neglected. [6] Although poems tend to be mentioned among the types of texts that fall within the scope of a possible-world semantics of fictionality (Dolezel 1989: 235–6; Wolterstoff 1980: 108, Maitre 1983: 10), they are rarely selected as the object of analysis (see Meneses 1991 for an exception). [7] The main reason for this neglect can be identified in the closeness of the link between possible-worlds' approaches to fiction and narrative analysis, which leads to privileged attention being devoted to texts with a strong narrative element, such as stories and novels. [8] In fact, some possible-world theorists have gone as far as arguing that, unlike prose fiction and drama, poetry does not involve the projection of fictional worlds, but rather the expression of moods, themes and atmospheres, which are not amenable to possible-world analysis. [9] In such cases it is lyric poetry in particular that is singled out as the mode of literary discourse that falls outside the boundaries of fictionality (Ryan 1991a: 83–87).[1] [10]

The aim of this paper is to demonstrate the relevance of possible-world frameworks to the study of poetic text worlds. [11] My argument will proceed as follows. [12] In the first part of the paper, I will briefly discuss the development of the notion of possible worlds from logic to the semantics of fictionality, and consider the way in which a possible-world approach can be used to describe and classify fictional worlds; I will focus particularly on the framework developed by Ryan (1991a, 1991b). [13] In the second part of the paper, I will show how possible-world models, and specifically Ryan's approach, can be applied to poetry. [14] In particular, I will adopt a possible-world perspective in order to consider:

    (i)   the internal structure of the world projected by a particular poem;

    (ii) the projection of deviant situations of address;

    (iii) the description of different types of poetic worlds. [15]

I will conclude with a discussion of the main weaknesses of possible-world frameworks, and with some suggestions for future developments in the study of text worlds. [16]

WRITING AN INTRODUCTION: ADDITIONAL STEPS

Outlining the Dissertation

An Introduction to a Type 1 dissertation often consists of only the four basic steps described above, before the literature review begins. However, in Type 2, 3 and 4 dissertations, one more step is essential. This is the step exemplified in Sentences 12 to 16 in the text in Task 1.1 above. These sentences give an outline of the organisation and content of the remainder of the paper. This preview of the remaining chapters prepares readers for what is to come. In a Type 1 dissertation this outline of contents comes at the end of Chapter 1, after the literature has been reviewed, rather than at the end of the Introduction. (We will return to the theme of using signals to prepare the reader in Chapter 5 on Signposting.)

Explaining the Reason for the Gap

Sentences 8 to 10 in the text in Task 1.1 explain the reason for the existing gap. This is not a common step in Introductions, but a writer may think that it is useful to give an explanation for why other researchers have not already examined the area that is to be explored, as such an explanation may help to justify the research which is to be undertaken. This step can be included in the Introduction to any type of dissertation and will come immediately after the gap has been identified.

Stating the Delimitations

Some Introductions have yet one more step and that is to indicate the delimitations (also known as 'scope') of the research. This step puts boundaries on the research and tells readers what the study will *not* cover. Where this step is included in the Introduction, it will appear immediately after basic step 4, when the purpose is stated. Such a step is only necessary where it is not already absolutely clear from the terminology used what the boundaries will be. If, for instance, you have stated that it is your purpose to establish whether or not there is a correlation between birth weight and the development of reading difficulties, you may need to delimit your study in order to clarify exactly who your subjects will be, as in the text below:

Example 1.2

1.6 Delimitations

My study will examine only babies who were carried to full-term before birth; babies born prematurely will not be included as premature babies may have added difficulties, such as breathing or feeding problems, which distinguish them from full-term babies, and this changed birth profile could complicate the picture. My study will also be confined to primary school children with reading difficulties who are within what is considered the normal IQ range for educational purposes; I will not include children whose IQ is deemed to be below normal as including these children in the study would introduce factors of intellectual development, which are outside the scope of this research.

In this section of the paper, the writer makes it clear what categories of babies (premature ones) and children (those with below 'normal' IQ) will not be studied and explains why they have not been included. Stating the delimitations clearly means that readers will not be misled about what to expect in the study.

WRITING AN INTRODUCTION: LANGUAGE FEATURES

We will focus on some of the language features that are important when introducing your research. To do this, we will examine the texts studied so far in this chapter. We will concentrate on what tense you should choose when taking the four basic steps identified earlier, plus the outlining step, and on the vocabulary that is common when indicating the research gap.

Tense

Step 1: Describe the problem/difficulty/situation that interests you

Extract	Comment
Pleomorphic adenoma *is* the most common salivary gland neoplasm and frequently *recurs* after simple surgical excision due to incomplete removal of its unencapsulated portion or to the presence of "satellite nodules". [1] (From Example 1.1)	The two tenses used are the *present simple*, as this is used to describe the present situation, and the *present perfect*, as this is used to bring us up to date with what has happened up until the present day.
Over the last couple of decades, the study of literary text worlds *has made* considerable advances under the influence of the possible-world frameworks originally developed within modal logic and logical semantics. [1] The notion of possible worlds, which *was devised* by philosophers and logicians to solve a number of logical problems, *has been* increasingly *extended* to provide a theoretical base for fundamental issues within the semantics of fictionality. [2] These *include* the logical properties of sentences of and about works of fiction, the ontological status of fictional entities, the definition of fiction, and the nature of the worlds projected by different types of fictional and/or literary text. [3] (From Task 1.1)	Note 1: The past simple is used only once ('was devised' in the text from Task 1.1) to describe a completed past event. Note 2: Both active and passive voice can be used, as appropriate.

Step 2: Establish what has been said and done in the area

Extract	Comment
Malignant change of the lesion *is known* to occur, although its incidence *is* frequently difficult to estimate when based solely on qualitative histopathological features. [2] It *is* generally *agreed* that the vast majority of these neoplasms *are* essentially benign, but the existence of locally malignant variants, or lesions with malignant potential, *has been described.* [3] Further, it *has been suggested* that truly malignant or semimalignant variants exist. [4] Flow cytometry (FC) *has* unique advantages for examining the DNA content of tumour cells and the technique *has been used* for diagnostic and prognostic assessment of a wide variety of tumours. [5] (From Example 1.1)	The tense that predominates is the *present perfect*, with some use of the *present simple*. This is, in fact, the tense that you would expect to use as this section is describing what has been done in the research area up to and including the present day.

More specifically, possible-world models *have been used* in order to:
(a) describe fictional worlds as complex modal structures made up of a central domain counting as actual and a number of secondary domains counting as non-actual (such as characters' belief worlds, wish worlds, fantasy worlds, etc.) (e.g. Eco 1979, 1990; Pavel 1986, Ryan 1991a);
(b) classify text worlds on the basis of the accessibility relations (Kripke 1971) that *link* them to the actual world, i.e. on the basis of criteria such as logical possibility, physical possibility, and so on (e.g. Maitre 1983, Ryan 1991a). [4]

The vast majority of possible-world approaches to the study of fiction *have focused* on literary narratives (e.g. Dolezel 1976a, 1976b; Maitre 1983, Ryan 1991a), with the occasional reference to drama (e.g. Pavel 1986). [5] (From Task 1.1)

Step 3: Point out the gap

Extract	Comment
However, reports of the application of FCM to salivary gland tumours *are* few and the number of cases studied in each report *have been* very limited. [6] (From Example 1.1) Poetry, on the other hand, *has been* largely *neglected*. [6] (From Task 1.1)	The *present perfect* and the *present simple* are used, although the former usually predominates. As with Step 2, the present perfect is to be expected as what is being described is what has not been done up to the present day.

Step 4: Explain what you hope to add to the body of knowledge

Extract	Comment
In the present study, we examined 10 pleomorphic adenomas from major salivary glands using FCM, with normal salivary glands and chronic sialadenitis lesion as control. [7] Our purpose *was* to examine the DNA content and proliferative patterns in the lesions in order to detect any possible correlations between FCM analysis, diagnosis and the biological behavior of these tumours. [8] (From Example 1.1) The aim of this paper *is* to demonstrate the relevance of possible world frameworks to the study of poetic text worlds. [11] (From Task 1.1)	This is a feature of Introductions where disciplines do tend to differ. Most use the *present simple* to state the aims of the research (as in the text in Task 1.1) but a few use the *past simple* (as in Example 1.1). Check the conventions in your field.

Last step: Outline/preview the content of the remainder of the dissertation

Extract	Comment
My argument *will proceed* as follows. [12] In the first part of the paper, I *will* briefly *discuss* the development of the notion of possible worlds from logic to the semantics of fictionality, and *consider* the way in which a possible-world approach can be used to describe and classify fictional worlds; I *will focus* particularly on the framework developed by Ryan (1991 a, 1991b). [13] In the second part of the paper, I *will show* how possible-world models, and specifically Ryan's approach, can be applied to poetry. [14] ... I *will conclude* with a discussion of the main weaknesses of possible-world frameworks, and with some suggestions for future developments in the study of text worlds. [16] (From Task 1.1)	The *future tense* is probably the most common for this step, on the basis that the rest of the content is yet to come, but many writers use the *present simple*, taking the view that at the time of reading, the content already exists.

Vocabulary

The gap

Note that the vocabulary used to indicate the gap in each text is chosen to stress what is missing:

    Example 1.1:   *reports of ... **are few** and the number of cases ... **have been very limited.***

    Task 1.1:   *Poetry ... **has been largely neglected** ... **they are rarely selected as** ...*

Take a look at texts in your own discipline and note the type of negative vocabulary that is common when stating the gap.

Signalling the gap

The sentence which introduces the gap usually has a signalling expression that leads the reader to expect that a contrast to the preceding text is about to be presented, i.e. what has not been done in contrast to what has been done. In our two texts we have the following:

Example 1.1:   *However, reports of the application of FCM ...*

Task 1:   *Poetry, **on the other hand**, has been largely neglected.*

The latter of these is not so common as 'however' and should be used with caution, as its applications are much narrower and it is not always appropriate. In this text it is only possible because the immediately preceding sentence specifically states what aspects of fiction possible-world approaches 'have focussed' on, so 'on the other hand' can be used to present the negative aspects of the situation.

Use of first person

You will have noticed that the literary semantics text (in Task 1.1) makes extensive use of the first person when outlining the remainder of the paper. This technique has become common practice in more recent years, at this point of the dissertation and in the conclusion. It is not well-liked in some disciplines though, which find the use of the first person too personal for an academic text. Alternative techniques are to use the passive voice or to make part of the text into the subject of the sentence. Using these techniques for Task 1.1, we would have:

1. In the first part of the paper, the development of the notion of possible worlds from logic to the semantics of fictionality *will be discussed,* and the way in which a possible-world approach can be used to describe and classify fictional worlds *will be considered;* the framework developed by Ryan *will be* particularly *focussed on* (1991 a, 1991b).

2. *The first part of the paper will discuss* the development of the notion of possible-worlds from logic to the semantics of

fictionality *and consider* the way in which a possible-world approach can be used to describe and classify fictional worlds; *the paper will focus* particularly on the framework developed by Ryan (1991 a, 1991b).

You should note that in version 1 above, the use of the passive leads to the sentences having extremely long subjects for the verbs, which is often considered rather poor style in English and can sound very awkward. You should bear this in mind when considering which technique to use.

Note:
It was common practice until recent years for a writer to refer to him/herself as 'this writer' or 'this author' in order to avoid using 'I'. This is now a very rare practice and is considered rather dated.

REVIEWING THE LITERATURE

In both the texts we have studied so far, the authors cite related work that has been done in the field. Sometimes in Type 1 dissertations no citations are actually made in the introduction, but the work of others is referred to indirectly by stating what is presently known and not known in the research area. The purpose of referring to the work of others at the introductory stage is only to inform readers of the situation that led to the research being undertaken. This is rather different from the purpose of reviewing the literature in the section/chapter called the Literature Review or Literature Survey, which usually comprises between one-quarter and one-third of your entire dissertation. The purpose of citing others at this stage is to **analyse** and **evaluate** what they have said and done to create the fundamental basis for your entire study. Reviewing the literature shows your readers that you are familiar with the previous work done in your field and it draws together different strands or aspects related to your proposed area of study. Through analysing and evaluating the work of others, you clarify the current state of knowledge and justify the research being conducted by showing what has not yet been done, i.e. where there remains a gap in knowledge.

This establishes a need for the research and shows that the study will, indeed, add something new to the existing body of knowledge.

For ease of reference, the following section of this chapter will refer to a literature review as a separate section/chapter of a dissertation. This is not, in fact, so in Type 3 dissertations. However, although the literature is not reviewed separately, each chapter can be viewed, to some extent, as a literature review in its own right. In discussing each topic or conducting a text analysis, what has been said or done by other researchers is analysed and evaluated to show how the writer's ideas fit in with and add to the current state of knowledge. This being so, most of the features of a literature review discussed below are relevant to all types of dissertations; where a feature is not applicable to a Type 3 dissertation, this will be noted.

If yours is a Type 4 dissertation, where each chapter after the Introduction, being a published paper in its own right, has its own literature review, what is said in this chapter about reviewing the literature should be read in conjunction with the advice at the end of the chapter on 'Introducing Academic Papers'.

To start you thinking about what you need to include in the literature review in order to successfully identify your gap, look at the following task:

TASK 1.2

The two extracts below are taken from examiners' reports. On the basis of these extracts, draw up a list of features that are expected from a good review of the literature.

Text 1

The literature review is as detailed and comprehensive as one could wish it to be. One feature of the review which was particularly pleasing was the way in which the candidate distinguished between substantive and methodological issues. This division makes a good deal of sense, although it is relatively uncommon in studies of this type.

Text 2

The literature on communication is large and growing, as the candidate points out, and this therefore makes an exhaustive review difficult, if not impossible. However, while Hymes and Labov, two of the seminal figures in the field, are referred to, other more recent contributions are not. In addition, I found three references in the body of the dissertation that do not appear in the list of references. I find the review is disorganised and unfocussed. The candidate provides us with a historical tour, rather than a treatment of the thematic concerns underlying his research. The overall effect of the literature review is a superficial piling up of results and facts with no summary statements at the end of sections to pull research findings together and to highlight significant trends.

Just as seriously, the analysis is descriptive rather than analytical. There is almost no critical analysis of some rather questionable studies, and little supporting evidence for controversial claims. The candidate does not explore the implications of the research, nor does he relate the research to his own. As a result, the purpose and justification for his own work are almost entirely absent.

KEY FEATURES OF A LITERATURE REVIEW

1. The literature review needs to be relevant and focussed.

In most fields it is impossible to cover all that has been written within the field. Hence, it is important that writers are selective in the works that they cite. Only those papers or studies that are directly relevant to one's study need to be included in the literature review and a direct relationship between the cited works and one's own study needs to be drawn.

2. The review needs to be organised thematically.

It may be necessary in some disciplines to give a brief history of the developments in the research area under study, for example, an historical account of various treatments used to cure a disease. However, the main body of the literature review should be organised around themes which relate to the overall study, rather than chronologically, as the latter type of organisation tends to lead to a great deal of repetition and also makes it difficult for readers to extract the main themes for themselves. This type of organisation may not be applicable to a Type 3 dissertation, where the organisation is dictated by the topic of each chapter.

3. The organisation should be signalled in an introductory paragraph.

You should not leap into reviewing the first study/author of relevance to your work. This is what has been done in the example below, taken from an early draft of an MPhil dissertation:

EXAMPLE 1.3.1

II.   Literature Review

IBD is an acute, highly contagious viral infection of young chickens that has lymphoid tissue as its primary target with a special predilection for the bursa of Fabricus (Luckert and Saif, 1997). It was first recognised as a specific disease entity in 1962 and was referred to as "avian nephrosis" because of the extreme kidney damage found in birds that succumbed to infection (Cosgrove, 1962).

The reader has no idea at the beginning of this review what is to come in terms of overall content or the relation of the parts to each other. What is missing is some background and/or signal as to what the review will consider in order to prepare readers for the content of the review. (This aspect of writing will be more fully discussed under 'Signposting' in Chapter 5.)

In Example 1.3.2 below, we can see how the addition of an introductory paragraph to Example 1.3.1 presents the reader with a preview of the literature review:

EXAMPLE 1.3.2

II.   **Literature Review**
In this literature review, I will first briefly introduce the importance of IBD. Then I will discuss the ineffectiveness of the current and DNA vaccines. After that, I will explain why edible vaccination is one of the possible ways to fight against IBD in Hong Kong.

II. I The importance of IBD
IBD is an acute, highly contagious viral infection of young chickens that has lymphoid tissue as its primary target with a special predilection for the bursa of Fabricus (Luckert and Saif, 1997). It was first recognised as a specific disease entity in 1962 and was referred to as "avian nephrosis" because of the extreme kidney damage found in birds that succumbed to infection (Cosgrove, 1962).

Notice how the introductory paragraph forms the organisational framework for the review. Writing such a paragraph should also help you as the writer to plan the thematic organisation of the text based on how the areas selected for review relate to your own study. In a Type 3 dissertation, each chapter will have its own introductory paragraph to signal how that chapter is organised.

TASK 1.3

Look at the two introductory paragraphs below, each taken from Chapter 2 of a postgraduate dissertation, and decide what you think the subheadings of the sections following the opening paragraph in the two literature reviews would be:

Text 1

Literature Review

Bone has three main functions: (a) it is a major organ for calcium homeostasis (b) bones provide mechanical support for the soft tissues and are levers for muscle action and (c) bone is the major site for hematopoiesis in the human adult. To fulfill these functions, bone is continuously broken down and rebuilt. When the breakdown and the formation of bone are not in balance, there is either bone loss or bone gain. Most diseases of the skeleton are due to such an imbalance. This section will focus on bone formation and remodeling, including recent advances. Finally, details about a mouse model with progressive hyperostosis will be discussed.

Text 2

Literature Review

In this chapter, approaches to style analysis will be introduced. Then its uses and applications will be discussed in detail. Following this will be a review of the construction of property price indices. Finally, the objectives and hypotheses of this study will be presented.

4. The literature review should be up to date.

How far back one goes depends very much on the area under investigation and on the extent of the field. There is no golden rule here. It may be necessary to refer to some seminal work reported a century ago. In the text on IBD (Examples 1.3.1 and 1.3.2), the writer goes back to 1962 *(Cosgrove, 1962)* as that was the first time that IBD was recognised as a specific disease. However, it is essential for the literature review to consider the most recent findings even if they are reported just before you are about to hand in your dissertation. Examiners do look at the references to see whether they are comprehensive and whether the researcher has continued to keep up to date right until the time of submission. If you were to submit your dissertation in 2005, but your most recent reference was 1999, the examiner would be likely to question when you had finished reading around your topic. If no more recent literature is available, which is possible, though rare, you would need to explain why this is the case. Perhaps, for example, after its discovery a theory was neglected because of difficulties in practical application due to technological limitations in previous years.

5. The literature review needs to be critical.

It is not sufficient for you to say 'who said what' and expect your readers to make the judgements as to the value of works you are citing. You generally need to indicate the relative importance of works you cite and where conflicts are reported, you need to adjudicate on whose findings you consider the most plausible. (The language with which you achieve this is considered in detail in Chapter 3.) Below we provide a number of examples to show how published writers make their reviews critical.

EXAMPLE 1.4

Research of a philosophical nature, including that of international scholars such as Reid (e.g. 1969), Best (e.g. 1974) and Redfern (e.g. 1983), has made an invaluable contribution to the clarification of fundamental concepts and continues to be entirely relevant, while the enduring influence in many countries of experts such as Brinson (1991) is also acknowledged (pp. 118–119).

EXAMPLE 1.5

The seminal 'Attitude to Physical Activity Inventory' developed by Kenyon (1986) is unusual in including an aesthetic attitude scale, although this is too general to have been of any significant value to dance researchers (pp. 121–122).

Notice that in the above two examples the author is making evaluative comments about previous research, but they are generally positive. In the next three examples the evaluative comments are negative.

EXAMPLE 1.6

Although the argument put forward by Alderson holds in that there is infinite variability of language which simulations can draw upon, it does not acknowledge the consequences of using simulations which may be far from trivial.

EXAMPLE 1.7

Bachman and Palmer fail to justify on what grounds they assert that test takers perceive authenticity as an important criterion. Indeed, both premises which underlie the researchers' notion of authenticity appear to be based on conjecture.

EXAMPLE 1.8

However, tea polyphenolics have been implicated in promoting carcinogenic effects.[238, 239] The report of Kaiser[238] is based on inadequate controls in experiments, while the report of Morton [239] is based on an epidemiological study which is rather speculative in nature.

6. The literature review needs to be brought to a close.

It is not sufficient to stop at the last work that is cited. You need to summarise the main points of the literature review at the end, drawing together the different themes that you have introduced. In fact, you need to summarise the information at fairly regular intervals in a dissertation, generally when you have completed the review of one theme and are about to move on to another. Example 1.9 below shows the summary at the end of a review section in a journal article, where the writers draw together the information gained from the review to make a conclusion about the variables involved in the area being studied:

EXAMPLE 1.9

> Based on this concise review, we may conclude that an MNL is frequently used in the literature to describe passengers' port or route choices. Variables of influence appear to be travel time (to the airport), frequency and airfare. It may be, however, that an NMNL is to be statistically preferred.

7. The research gap should arise from the literature review.

From your analysis of the literature, it should have become apparent that there are certain limitations in previous research or certain areas that have not yet been studied fully, or, indeed, that have not been studied at all. When you have finished your review, you need to explicitly state what is missing from the previous studies to explain what your study intends to do to fill the gap.

TASK 1.4

Look at the two texts below where the writers identify their research gaps and answer the following questions:

1. What limitations in the previous research do the writers point out?
2. What are the researchers going to do to fill the gaps in knowledge?
3. What do the researchers do to justify their assumption that the gap should be filled?
4. In Text 2, what is the purpose of the second paragraph?

Text 1

The sparse data available on prepubertal children's responses to aerobic and anaerobic exercise training are both conflicting and limited by samples of only boys or mixed groups of boys and girls. The lack of data on young girls' responses to exercise training is particularly unfortunate because it is well documented that significant differences exist in aerobic and anaerobic performance of prepubescent boys and girls [references given]. This study was therefore designed to investigate the effects of exercise training on the aerobic and anaerobic performance of prepubescent girls. More specifically, the study examined the effects of a cycle ergometer training programme, which could be regarded as mainly anaerobic training, on the aerobic power (peak VO_2) and anaerobic performance (peak power in 5 s and mean power over 30 s) of girls classified as Tanner stage 1 (prepubertal) for sexual maturity [reference given].

Text 2

2.4 Aims and Hypotheses

As shown in section 2.2, few studies of style analysis have been in the real estate field and, even where these do exist, their applications have been limited to property funds only. In fact, a property company, like a property fund, would normally hold a portfolio of properties as well as other intangible assets, like stocks and cash. To manage these assets, there is a need for asset allocation. Therefore, it is argued that if style analysis can be applied to property funds, it should be equally applicable to property companies. Based on this logic, this study attempts to identify the investment styles of property companies in Hong Kong through style analysis and then to evaluate their performance relative to their style benchmarks.

To achieve these aims, there are two prerequisites. One is the construction of appropriate price indices. As pointed out in section 2.3, while the issue is still controversial, most of the literature has leant more support towards the repeat-sales approach than to the hedonic approach. Hence, this study will construct property price indices using a repeat-sales method. The other pre-requisite is the choice of style analysis approach. This study will use the returns-based approach, which is the most favoured in the literature discussed in section 2.1.

THE LITERATURE REVIEW: AN ADDITIONAL FEATURE

If you construct your literature review as outlined above, you will have clearly explained to your readers what the current state of knowledge is in your research area, clarified precisely where the gap is and stated what you intend to do to fill the gap. However, in some dissertations, there is one more step to be taken before the literature review is complete: you need to state your hypotheses or research questions. The placement of this section tends to be rather discipline-specific and this is something you should check; the section always precedes the description of how you conducted your research, but it may come after all the introductory material, i.e. after you have completed your review of the literature in a Type 1 or 2 dissertation, or at the end of the introductory chapter in a Type 3 dissertation. Alternatively, it may come at the beginning of the Methods section. In a Type 4 dissertation, the hypotheses will appear in each individual chapter or article. Wherever the hypotheses/research questions are placed, they must arise from what is already known and be related to the gap you have identified.

Hypotheses and Research Questions

Hypotheses

Whether you state a hypothesis or ask a research question depends upon the type of research that you are doing. If you are conducting purely experimental, quantitative research, where the knowledge acquired from studies conducted previously has led you to expect a certain relationship to exist between two or more variables, you are in a position to state a hypothesis, i.e. to make an assumption based on what is already known. The purpose of your research then is to find out if your hypothesis is supported or not. It is always important to remember that you are setting out to *test* and *not to prove* the truth of the assumption you have made.

A hypothesis must have the following characteristics:

1. a specific/directional relationship posited between two or more variables;
2. unambiguous variables;
3. a relationship that can be empirically tested.

Here are two examples of hypotheses:

(a) Drug X causes nausea and migraines when used for a period of more than 6 weeks.
(b) Sex education classes in the upper forms of secondary school decrease the incidence of sexually transmitted diseases amongst the students.

Note that the verb tense used when stating a hypothesis is the present simple because you are stating the assumed relationship in the sentence as a fact, not as a prediction or condition.

TASK 1.5

Look at the four statements below, which appeared as hypotheses at the end of the literature review in Text 2 of Task 1.4. Decide if you think all four of these statements have the characteristics necessary for hypotheses.

The hypotheses of the study are:

i) The performance of property companies leads that of the property market;

ii) The implied direct property allocations of each company should not be statistically different from that of actual allocations;

iii) The larger the market size of a property company is, the more (less) this company outperforms (underperforms) its style benchmark;

iv) The higher the gearing ratio a property company maintains, the less (more) this company outperforms (underperforms) its style benchmark.

Research questions

If you are carrying out qualitative, exploratory research or conducting a study which has both qualitative and quantitative aspects, it may not be possible to state a hypothesis; there may be insufficient evidence from the existing studies to allow you to assume a definite relationship between the variables you are interested in. In this case, you must pose a research question that you wish to answer. The purpose of your research then is to find the answer to the question. You are not testing an assumption, as with a hypothesis, but making a discovery. For example, if you have no idea what the side effects of a drug that you are testing might be, you will want to ask the following question:

What are the potential side effects of drug X?

Or you may want to distinguish between short-term and long-term effects, so you will have two separate questions:

1. What are the potential side effects of drug X when used for no more than two weeks?
2. What are the potential side effects of drug X when used for long term therapy?

The nature of a research question means that it allows for a wide range of answers, unlike a hypothesis, which can only be supported or unsupported.

Turning a hypothesis into a question

You should note that it is always possible to reformulate a hypothesis as a research question; for example, the two hypotheses given as examples above:

(a) Drug X causes nausea and migraines when used for a period of more than 6 weeks.
(b) Sex education classes in the upper forms of secondary school decrease the incidence of sexually transmitted diseases amongst the students.

could be rewritten as:

(c) Does drug X cause nausea and migraines when used for a period of more than 6 weeks?
(d) Do sex education classes in the upper forms of secondary school decrease the incidence of sexually transmitted diseases amongst the students?

However, some disciplines do not adopt this practice and insist that students always state a hypothesis that will be tested in their research. You should check what the convention is in your field.

TASK 1.6

In Text 1 of Task 1.4 above, what do you think were the research questions that the researchers investigated?

Bringing It All Together

Points to remember:

❖ Although the introduction is the first part of your dissertation that readers will see, the final version of it is usually one of the last parts that is written. You will probably have written an early draft when you began your research to clarify for yourself the context in which you were carrying out your research. However, it is only when you have finished your study that you have a clear picture of the whole process to be able to easily summarise what was known and not known before the actual writing of the dissertation. Therefore, your introduction will not be finalised until the research has been completed.

❖ As all your readers, apart from your supervisor, come to your dissertation with no prior knowledge of your aims, it is essential that the introductory material, i.e. the introduction and literature review, should set the scene for the research by answering the questions: *What?* and *Why?*

❖ Your literature review should be analytical, not purely descriptive.

❖ Your literature review should:
   • have a clear introduction;
   • be up to date;
   • be thematically organised;
   • regularly summarise the important information;
   • draw all the information together at the end.

❖ The research gap should grow out of the limitations of the previous research.

❖ The research questions/hypotheses should arise from what has been already established in the field.

Introducing Academic Papers

A major difference between an academic paper and a dissertation is one of focus: the focus of a paper will inevitably be narrower. If the paper is based on research you carried out for your dissertation, you are likely to select one aspect or topic covered in your dissertation, rather than try to summarise the whole dissertation in a single paper.

The narrower focus of an academic paper will affect what you include in the introductory section of your paper and particularly the amount of detail you include in your literature review. However, as we have seen in the examples taken from journal articles earlier in this chapter, the structure of the introductory sections of both journal articles and dissertations is very similar. The introduction is the point at which you need to engage your audience and interest them. In it you will:

- provide relevant background;
- identify the need for your research;
- specify clearly what problem or issue you are researching;
- signal the organisation for your text.

It is important that you keep this section succinct and to the point. With the limit imposed by most journals on the length of a paper, you need to balance the introductory section with the rest of the paper.

The literature review will need to relate only to the problem or issue being addressed in the article, thus it will be considerably shorter than in a dissertation. It will most probably form part of the introduction rather than be a separate section (though this will depend on the subject-matter of the paper). The primary purpose of the literature review of a paper is to show an awareness of what has been done in the field you are reporting on in order to show there is a need for your research. This will help to identify the contribution you are making to the field.

Further Advice

As you are reading papers in your area, note how these published articles introduce their work and how they identify their research gap clearly through the introduction and literature review. Look at some dissertations in your field as well and decide which type of organisation tends to prevail.

Follow-up Tasks

1. Choose two or three academic papers in your field on one of the themes that you will cover in your dissertation and write an introduction to a review of those papers.
2. Identify an article or dissertation related to your research area and analyse the introduction in terms of the steps discussed in this chapter.
3. Look at the literature review section/chapter of two or three dissertations in your field. Analyse to what extent the reviews meet the requirements expected of a good literature review in terms of the key features introduced in this chapter.

2 Making Use of Source Materials

As we have seen in Chapter 1, it is essential when writing a dissertation to refer to other scholars whose work you have used for source material during your research. References to the work of other scholars appear throughout a dissertation, although they are, naturally, most frequent when actually reviewing the literature. As making references to your sources is such an important element in your dissertation, this chapter aims to consider the reasons a writer has for referring to the work of others and looks at different methods of referring, before examining the language that is used to make these references.

REASONS FOR REFERRING

You may have a variety of reasons for referring to the work of others, but there are two reasons which underlie all other. We will discuss these first and then move on to consider other reasons.

1. To Avoid Being Accused of Plagiarism

The need to acknowledge the work and ideas of others in order not to be accused of plagiarism clearly applies to each and every instance of making a reference. It is vitally important that you should give full credit to those who have done/are doing work in your field and one way of doing this is through referring to these people in your writing. This is not only a matter of academic courtesy, but an ethical and legal issue.

2. To Demonstrate Familiarity with the Field

Another reason for citing others that underlies all citations is the need to demonstrate familiarity with the field in order to establish your membership of a particular academic community. You can consider that the situation is rather like joining a club for experts. To become a member you need to show that you share the interests of the other members; you want the other members, i.e. your readers, to know that you are familiar with what has been said on the topic being investigated, that you have read what you should have read if you wish to be considered an expert. Below are two examples of references made for this reason.

EXAMPLE 2.1

Casanave and Hubbard (1992) stated that supervisors of postgraduate students at Stanford University rated spelling and punctuation quite low on the scale of items affecting their grading.

EXAMPLE 2.2

Students in a study by Parkhurst (1990) indicated that to improve their style they adopted a strategy of reading extensively and imitating what they had read.

The writer of these examples is merely showing an awareness of what else has been written in the area being researched. In neither of the examples does the writer express an opinion about the research reported; there is no analysis or evaluation of the works cited. The writer's reason for citing here is only to demonstrate familiarity with the field.

3. To Show Your Support for or to Refute the Work of Other Researchers

Frequently, however, it is not sufficient only to report what has been done and to remain neutral towards the research. You need to evaluate the work of others in order to negotiate your position with regard to the present body of knowledge and to establish your stance. This then is another reason for referring to background sources. Below are three examples of references made for this purpose.

EXAMPLE 2.3

Smith (1995) presents a convincing argument in favour of introducing legislation to legalise soft drugs.

EXAMPLE 2.4

Innovative research by Yang et al. (1999) demonstrates that there is a significant correlation between the mother's age at birth and increased risk of birth defects.

EXAMPLE 2.5

According to Clark (1991) the students in his survey found the use of the passive voice to be the most difficult grammatical feature to master. However, he fails to explain why the student samples that he cites do not exhibit errors with this aspect of writing. This is further evidence of the unreliability of his findings.

Example 2.3 gives a clear idea of the writer's positive attitude towards the research by the use of *'presents a convincing argument'*. Example 2.4 also makes it clear that the writer is praising the research referred to by the use of the positive adjective *'innovative'* and a reporting verb that indicates that strong evidence was provided, i.e. *'demonstrates'*. In these two examples the writers are supporting the research cited. By contrast, Example 2.5 gives just as clear an idea of the writer's negative evaluation of another researcher's work, with '*he fails to explain*' and '*the unreliability of his findings*'. Such overt negative comments, though sometimes necessary, are, in fact, relatively rare in dissertations and should be presented with caution; you must be very sure of your ground if you intend to criticise someone else's work.

4. To Support Your Own Findings

References to your sources are not, of course, confined to the introduction and literature review. When discussing your results, it is also essential for your findings to be related to the work of others, the main reason being to give support to your own findings and, thereby, give more authority to your statements. You want your readers to know that your findings are not peculiar to your research, but are in tune with the findings of other researchers. Below are two examples of references made for this reason.

EXAMPLE 2.6

The results of our investigation showed that errors of spelling and punctuation were not considered by supervisors to be significant as they rarely obscured meaning. This finding is confirmed by Casanave and Hubbard (1992) who point out that supervisors of postgraduate students at Stanford University rated spelling and punctuation quite low on the scale of items affecting their grading.

EXAMPLE 2.7

Students in a study by Parkhurst (1990) noted that to improve their style they adopted a strategy of reading extensively and imitating what they had read. This suggests that the strategy that we intend to adopt in our new course, where students will be encouraged to consciously examine source texts before they complete their writing tasks, should be well received.

In Example 2.6 the writer has used a reference to the work of authority figures to back-up his/her own findings, while in Example 2.7 the writer has used another reference to support an intended course of action.

Relating your findings to those of others may, of course, necessitate your criticising the work of other researchers in the light of your own findings, just as you may have needed to negatively evaluate other people's research when reviewing the literature. Below is an example of how this can be done.

EXAMPLE 2.8

None of the respondents in the three surveys conducted in the present study reported the type of reactions noted by Smith (1993) in his research, which seems to suggest that Smith's perceptions were based on conjecture rather than reported accounts.

It should again be emphasised, as was mentioned earlier, that criticisms of others, although essential on occasions, are fairly uncommon and must be accompanied by sound evidence if they are to stand up to scrutiny. Criticisms tend to be more common in dissertations than in journal articles as the writer of a dissertation, in claiming expertise on a subject, should be in a stronger position to question the findings of others.

5. To Create a Research Space

The final reason for citing others is the one discussed at length in Chapter 1, that is, to create a research space by showing what has already been done in order to identify what has not been done in your area. This is the cumulative reason for the citations in the introduction to your research and when you review the literature in the field. We have seen several examples of citations used for this reason in Chapter 1. You are advised to refer back to these if you feel you need to revise this type of referencing.

TASK 2.1

Examine the extracts below, which are all taken from a journal article on speech and language performance of brain-injured children. Identify where the authors have referred to their sources and consider, apart from demonstrating familiarity and avoiding plagiarism, what their reasons are for making the references.

Extract 1

In fact, much of the existing research has used an all-inclusive approach to subject recruitment, which has resulted in the inclusion of a diverse range of aetiologies within a single experimental group. Ozanne and Murdoch (1990) considered that such methodological limitations as the use of experimental groups of mixed pathology, have prevented the identification of definite profiles of the linguistic characteristics of acquired childhood aphasia. Similarly, Dennis (1988) is critical of this all-inclusive approach to brain pathologies of different origins, and suggests that one way to attempt to understand the role of pathology in later language function over early brain damage is the careful comparison of different pathologies within the broader category of childhood brain damage. The present paper, therefore, tried to evaluate the speech and language skills of three groups of children who had suffered different forms of brain insult or injury: closed-head-injured children (CHI), children treated for acute lymphoblastic leukemia (ALL), and children treated for posterior Fossa tumour (PFT), with a view to establishing profiles of linguistic impairment according to underlying pathology.

Extract 2

... it may be that the observed generalized linguistic impairment reflects a generalized cognitive or intellectual decline, rather than a specific impairment in the linguistic domain. Such a decline in intellectual ability has frequently been documented in the past for each of these groups of children studied (Appleton et al. 1990, Chadwick et al. 1981a, b, Dalby and Obrzut 1991, Fletcher and Levin 1988, Gerry-Taylor et al. 1987, Levin and Eisenberg 1979, Pfefferbaum-Levine et al. 1984, Sue et al. 1990, Winogran et al. 1984).

Extract 3

… it is possible that the tasks included in the assessment failed to provide a sensitive enough measure of specific deficit areas, despite identifying a generalized decline in linguistic performance. Perhaps the inclusion of more specific assessment tasks similar to the experimental measures often used with brain-damaged adults (for example Caplan and Hildebrandt 1988, Kay et al. 1992), would highlight specific deficit areas attributable to the different aetiologies studied in the present experiment.

Extract 4

Closed-head-injured subjects in the present study had experienced a severe head injury, indicating a significant compromise of brain function involving the presence of coma for some time post-injury. In addition to the primary neurological effects of the brain injury, CHI children also typically experience secondary complications such as increased intracranial pressure and massive brain swelling in the first 24 hours post-injury (Bruce 1983). In contrast to the CHI children, the children undergoing treatment for PFT experienced primarily focal lesions in non-language areas. Secondary consequences of PFT, however, cannot be dismissed, and include diffuse effects such as hydrocephalus, and the diffuse effects of CNS prophylaxis. Indeed, Hudson et al. (1989) report that "even though the site of these tumours (PFT) would not in itself lead to the prediction of an associated language deficit, there are a number of factors occurring secondary to the presence and removal of posterior fossa tumours that could conceivably disturb language function"(p. 2).

METHODS OF REFERRING

There are a number of different methods of citation that are used in academic writing. It is quite common to place the name of the researcher(s) cited in parenthesis after the reference (see examples in Extracts 2, 3, 4 in Task 2.1). This method is particularly common when the writer wishes only to demonstrate familiarity with that work and is not making any evaluation of the research. In fact, bracketed references generally indicate the writer's acceptance of the facts stated in the citation. The same is true where a citation takes the form of a bracketed number or superscript. We can see this in the examples below:

EXAMPLE 2.9

The presence of these tumours almost invariably leads to hearing loss (Bruce, 2000).

EXAMPLE 2.10

The presence of these tumours almost invariably leads to hearing loss (2).

EXAMPLE 2.11

The presence of these tumours almost invariably leads to hearing loss.[2]

All three examples are referring to a paper written by Bruce in the year 2000 and are accepting the veracity of her findings.

Another method of citation is to preface the reference by '*According to + name of researcher*'. This method is also commonly employed just to demonstrate familiarity with certain sources as in Example 2.12 below.

EXAMPLE 2.12

According to Bruce (2000) the presence of these tumours almost invariably leads to hearing loss.

This type of reference can, however, be the prelude to a subsequent evaluation, as in Examples 2.13 and 2.14.

EXAMPLE 2.13

According to Bruce (2000), the presence of these tumours almost invariably leads to hearing loss. Her study provides the strongest evidence to date of this relationship.

EXAMPLE 2.14

According to Bruce (2000), the presence of these tumours almost invariably leads to hearing loss. However, her study groups were poorly defined and the sample size was far too small to be able to make such broad generalizations.

The methods of citation in these examples are all extremely common in journal articles and require no consideration of language choice. They are, however, far less common (though this varies with discipline) in a dissertation. This is because they do not allow for the subtle shades of meaning and optimum level of informativity that the use of reporting verbs can convey. When reporting verbs are used, the citations are known as **integrated citations**, that is to say, the researcher referred to is the subject of the sentence in which the reference is made. The next section will look in detail at the verbs used in integrated citations, as the choice of verb here is one of the most important language choices that you need to make when referring to your sources.

REFERRING TO SOURCES: LANGUAGE FEATURES

Choice of Verb

The reporting verbs used in integrated citations have to be carefully chosen as they can convey a great deal of information to the reader. One piece of information they can convey is:

the writer's attitude to the research being reported.

The verb chosen can indicate to the reader the attitude the writer is adopting in relation to the information reported, that is to say, the writer's stance in relation to the research. Where the writer wishes only to demonstrate familiarity and not to evaluate the research reported or indicate a position of acceptance or refutation in relation to the findings, he/she will adopt a neutral stance. Some of the verbs that can be used to indicate neutrality towards a source are shown in the examples given below.

EXAMPLE 2.15

Brown (1990) *noted* that children under the age of two were unaffected by the separation of their parents.

EXAMPLE 2.16

Lee (1990) *stated* that even children as young as eight months old were disturbed by the separation of their parents.

These two examples report only what the researchers said/wrote about their findings, without any comment from the writer. If these findings were reported in the same dissertation, both of the verbs might well be replaced by 'argued' or by 'contended' to stress that there had been a conflict or debate on this issue. We would then have:

EXAMPLE 2.17

Brown (1990) *argued* that children under the age of two were unaffected by the separation of their parents. Lee (1990), however, *contended* that even children as young as eight months old were disturbed by the separation of their parents.

It would not, however, be possible to report neutrally on both pieces of research as they contradict one another; the writer would need to adjudicate between these conflicting findings. The writer should choose a verb to indicate his/her position towards the research. If the writer reporting on these findings supported Lee, the following example would show this clearly.

EXAMPLE 2.18

Brown (1990) *claimed* that children under the age of two were unaffected by the separation of their parents, but Lee's (1990) research *established* that even children as young as eight months old were disturbed by such an event.

The choice of the verb *'claimed'* usually indicates that the writer is rather doubtful about the findings or at least does not find them truly convincing. The choice of the verb *'established'* to refer to Lee's work indicates to the reader that the writer is convinced by those findings rather than Brown's.

Other information that can be conveyed to the reader by the reporting verb is:

the original researcher's attitude to his/her own research.

The verb can inform the reader about the position, or stance, the researcher being referred to took towards his/her own research. The following three examples show the same findings being reported with a different verb used each time.

EXAMPLE 2.19

Graham (1987) *suggested* that television viewing of more than three hours per night adversely affects marital relations.

EXAMPLE 2.20

Graham (1987) *asserted* that television viewing of more than three hours per night adversely affects marital relations.

EXAMPLE 2.21

Graham (1987) *admitted* that television viewing of more than three hours per night adversely affects marital relations.

It is clear that in Example 2.19 Graham is less sure of his findings than in Example 2.20. Perhaps in 2.19 he was reporting on the results of a pilot study or the early stages of his research, whereas in 2.20 he had conducted sufficient research to be quite sure of his claims. By contrast in Example 2.21, with *'admitted'*, Graham is acknowledging his findings reluctantly. This implies that he did not originally accept the truth of the relationship being reported; maybe he is admitting that his hypothesis was not supported. A careless choice of verb may not convey the true attitude of the original researcher and could, in some cases, mislead the reader. If, for example, a writer used the sentence in Example 2.20, with the verb *'asserted'*, when Graham had, in fact, made it quite clear that he was reporting on his early studies, he would be entitled to object to being misrepresented as he had not claimed to have proof of the relationship being investigated. It is important here to realise that verbs indicating 'proof' of a situation or relationship need to be used with extreme care, particularly in the humanities and social sciences where real *proof* is often difficult to establish.

Note:
The most common reporting verb in the English language, 'say', is rarely used in academic writing. This is not because it is so neutral, giving no indication of the stance of the writer of the paper or the original researcher ('state' is just as neutral), but purely because it is conversational and, therefore, considered to be very informal.

TASK 2.2

Examine the two extracts below, which are taken from the introduction to an article in an architecture journal. Identify the reporting verbs and consider what the choice of verb tells the reader about the writers' attitude to the research being reported or the original researchers' attitude to their own research.

Extract 1

Although numerous analysts have speculated about the relationship between residential architecture, the use of space, and changing gender patterns within married households, only a few researchers have empirically investigated these connections (Kent, 1990; Lawrence, 1979; Tognoli, 1980). In one study, Kent (1984) asserted that among Western Europeans and North Americans, the use of space in kitchens is consistently restricted to food preparation and related clean-up tasks. European and North American kitchens also tend to be predominantly gender specific and used mainly by women. Hasell and Peatross (1990), in an analysis of American house plans built between 1945 and 1990, found that interior spatial layouts had changed significantly over the years. For example, kitchens were enlarged and walls became merely partial walls, or indeed completely disappeared in order to open the kitchens to the social centers of the house. Most researchers acknowledge that in addition to physical design changes, important changes have also been seen over the last 20 years in the meaning of the home (Csikszentmihalyi et al., 1981; Madigan, et al., 1990; Rapaport, 1982; Saegert, et al., 1980; Rocke, et al., 1980.)

Extract 2

Social, psychological, and behavioral changes not only influence, but are influenced by, spatial arrangements (Anthony, et al., 1990). As men's and women's lives converge (more women work outside the home, more men take part in household affairs), then their choices of space will not only vary from traditionally accepted arrangements but, indeed, may also converge. Theoretical links between changes in house design, gender, and family ideology have been studied by a number of researchers (c.f. Daunton, 1983; Franck, et al., 1989; Rock, et al., 1980; Thompson, 1982). Matrix (1984), for example, showed that Victorian townhouses reflected the internal hierarchy of the bourgeois family — the public 'masculine' parlor was located at the front of the house, while the private 'feminine' kitchen was located in the rear. Fox (1986) attempted to link post World War II social and economic changes with transformations in family relations and suburban houses.

TASK 2.3

When you use bracketed names as a citation method, they are not arranged randomly; there should be an organising principle for the list of names and this should be consistent throughout your dissertation.

(a) Look at the bracketed citations in the extracts in Task 2.2 and say what you think is the organising principle for the lists of names.

(b) Is this principle adhered to here in each list?

(c) What other organising principle could you use?

(d) What is the meaning of *c.f.* at the beginning of the list in Extract 2?

(e) Is the punctuation of *c.f.* correct?

(f) In what circumstances is *et al.* used?

(g) Is the punctuation in the citations which use *et al.* in Task 2.2 correct?

Adjectives and Adverbs

One more way that writers can indicate their opinion of source materials to the reader is through the use of adjectives and adverbs. These can be usefully employed on occasion, but they should not be overused. Below are three examples.

EXAMPLE 2.22

Quite *originally* (although not completely at variance with previous definitions), Myers (1989) basing his discussions on Brown and Levison's (1978) work argues that hedges can be better understood as positive or negative politeness strategies.

EXAMPLE 2.23

A *truly innovative* approach was taken by Murakami (1981) and it yielded *impressive* results.

EXAMPLE 2.24

> Cabot and Parker's 1964 *landmark* study was followed by an *uninspiring* series of studies by Grey (1966, 68, 69), which seriously lacked methodological rigour.

A word of warning!

The use of these terms varies considerably from discipline to discipline; an adjective that one field may use to praise research as 'good' may be used in another field to evaluate research as merely 'average'. This is one area where it is critical to examine texts in your own discipline and use the vocabulary according to the conventions.

It should also be noted that emotional and colloquial terms, such as 'brilliant', 'wonderful', 'dreadful', 'awful', must be avoided as such evaluations are inappropriate to an academic context. To help you decide if an adjective is appropriate or not, ask yourself, 'Could I use this word to describe a view from a mountain top or a film I've seen?' If the answer is 'Yes', then the word is unlikely to be appropriate in academic writing.

Note:

It is, of course, possible to combine the use of reporting verbs and/ or adjectives and adverbs with other methods of citation. In the examples below, taken from a paper on genetic screening, the writers combine integrated citations with a numbering system. The references at the end of the paper are arranged numerically in the order in which they appear in the paper, but reporting verbs, adjectives and adverbs are also used to show the writers' attitudes towards the research they are describing.

EXAMPLE 2.25

> Hershey and Chase[1] *showed definitively* that it was DNA that carried the genetic information.

EXAMPLE 2.26

Several techniques to sequence nucleotides in DNA were devised, *the most useful being* the Sanger dideooxynucleotide method described in 1977.[3]

Verb Tense

Another factor that a writer has to consider when referring to source texts is which tense of the verb to use. The choice of tense is generally between the present simple, the past simple and the present perfect as other tenses are used only infrequently in a dissertation. There are, in fact, few fixed rules about the use of tense when referring to sources, particularly when choosing between the past and present simple. This is one area where different disciplines seem to have a preference for using one or the other of these tenses for the reporting verb. There are, however, tendencies which cross disciplines and certain situations where the incorrect choice of verb tense can lead to ambiguity. This section will look at the use of the past and present simple and the present perfect when referring to the literature you are reviewing.

Referring to what was done in a single study or series of studies

Telling readers about an action in a study is no different from reporting any other completed event. If you wrote a letter to a friend one evening and mentioned what you had done that morning, you would write, 'I watched a film about Paris this morning and then I went for a swim.' The verbs are both in the past simple because the time when the actions took place, i.e. that morning, is completely over at the time of writing. The same situation applies to describing actions that took place in studies that were conducted before the time of writing. Below are two examples to illustrate this point:

Example 2.27

> Thompson and Moon (1996) *analysed* 64 texts written in French by native speakers of the language, using the criteria employed in Devis's earlier research.

Example 2.28

> In their research Gibson et al. (1988) *interviewed* 100 patients hospitalized after a heart attack.

In both of these examples, what the researchers actually did is being reported and the use of the past simple is a necessity; using the present simple in Example 2.27 would have indicated that the texts are analysed, and in Example 2.28 that the patients are interviewed, on a regular basis rather than during the time (now over) when the research was being carried out. However, if you wish to refer to what was said or written in the articles in which the original researchers reported the results of their studies, the past simple would not then be compulsory as we will demonstrate in the section below.

Referring to what was said/written by another researcher

When you are referring to what was said or written by other researchers, rather than describing what was actually done in their research, the choice of tense is more flexible. Both past and present simple can be used. Your choice depends on how you view a document that you read. You may view what is written as a completed event, i.e. the actual writing of the paper/dissertation is now over, in which case you will use the past simple. However, you can consider the paper/dissertation as a source of information that now exists and will continue to exist, in which case you will choose the present simple. The following examples show how the references in Examples 2.27 and 2.28 could have been written if what was *said* in the papers in which the studies were first reported was being referred to, rather than what was actually *done* in the research:

EXAMPLE 2.27.1

Thompson and Moon (1996) *point out* that an analysis of 64 texts written in French by native speakers of the language produced results contrary to Devis's earlier research.

EXAMPLE 2.27.2

Thompson and Moon (1996) *pointed out* that an analysis of 64 texts written in French by native speakers of the language, produced results contrary to Devis's earlier research.

EXAMPLE 2.28.1

Gibson et al. (1988), for example, *describe* a study where 100 patients hospitalized after a heart attack were interviewed.

EXAMPLE 2.28.2

Gibson et al. (1988), for example, *described* a study where 100 patients hospitalized after a heart attack were interviewed.

Both versions of each example are acceptable. Some disciplines, however, have a distinct preference for using one tense or the other when referring to a paper; you should look carefully at writing in your own discipline to see if this is the case and follow the conventions. Actually, it is common to find both past and present simple used within one paragraph without creating any misunderstandings. Some writers like to vary the tense to avoid monotony. However, there are occasions when it is advisable to deliberately use one tense rather than the other to accurately reflect the present state of affairs in the world and we will now look at a situation where this is important.

Conveying the present state of a debate in the field

When reviewing the literature in your field you may need to refer to a debate that is currently taking place or to a debate that took place in the past but has now been settled. In this case, your choice of tense should accurately reflect the situation as it is when you are writing. In the example below, the use of the present tense leaves the reader in no doubt that an issue is still being debated and no consensus has been reached:

EXAMPLE 2.29

> Boot camps are controversial for a variety of reasons (MacKenzie and Parent, 1992; Meachum, 1990). Some *worry* that it *is* naïve to expect a short term in a boot camp prison to be effective at changing offenders, while others *argue* that such institutions represent a return to earlier militaristic prisons. Morash and Rucker (1990) *contend* that aspects of the boot camps may actually inflict damage on participants.

Example 2.30 makes it equally clear that the debate being referred to is no longer current.

EXAMPLE 2.30

> The first, and most widely accepted, view *associated* the condition with inadequate parenting in the early years (Green, 1978; Lester, 1982; Crocker, 1984; Allcock, 1986). Others, most notably, Tenett (1982) and Greysmith (1984), *maintained* that trauma at birth was the most likely cause of such behaviour, while a small, yet quite influential group, led by Gorton and Panter (1985) *argued* that there was evidence to suggest a chemical imbalance in the brain of those suffering from the condition. Over the following decade Gorton and Panter's view *was adopted* by the vast majority of practitioners.

It is advisable to make this distinction quite clear even when this involves changing from the tense you generally use for referring to what has been written (if you have a preference, that is) as you will then avoid any ambiguity as to the currency of the debate.

Referring to a whole area of study

When referring to a whole area of study, rather than any specific work in that area, you are generally introducing readers to the present state of affairs arising from what has been done before the present day. The present perfect is the usual tense to use in such circumstances, as one of its main functions is to tie past actions to a present situation. In choosing the present perfect to refer to an area of study, you wish to show that, although certain particular studies are now finished, the area being studied is still under investigation and has present-day relevance. Sentences using the present perfect are generally found at the beginning of paragraphs and sections in a journal article or dissertation, where a topic is introduced in general before specific examples are given. This can be clearly seen in the following examples.

EXAMPLE 2.31

Theoretical Background
Research by sociologists into the citation practices in engineering *has revealed* that engineers' citations are meant to give credit for previous work, to pay intellectual debts, and to make new knowledge claims (Lau, 1989; Mellor et al., 1965; Tolkien, 1953). Lau's paper points out that acknowledging your debt to your predecessors in the field is a fundamental tenet of academic life, although she admits not all researchers adhere scrupulously to ethical practices.

EXAMPLE 2.32

Revision in Learning Academic Writing
Studies of composition revision *have expanded* to investigations of how professors revise their students' writing in different content areas (Beason, 1993; Herrington, 1985; McCarthy, 1987; Prior, 1991, 1995). Herrington's profile of two American students in a writing course in anthropology illustrated how the students learned to interact with the instructor and learned to talk like an insider in the discipline.

EXAMPLE 2.33

Personal Characteristics and Creativity

As noted earlier, a large body of literature *has focused* on determining a set of personal characteristics and attributes associated with creative achievement (Barron & Harrington, 1981; Davis, 1989; Martindale, 1989). This research *has examined* personal characteristics ranging from biographical factors to measures of cognitive styles and intelligence (Amabile, 1983; Barron & Harrington, 1981; Davis, 1989; Hocevar & Bachelor, 1989; Woodman & Schoenfeldt, 1989). In general, these studies *have demonstrated* that a stable set of core personal characteristics, including broad interests, attraction to complexity, intuition, aesthetic sensitivity, toleration of ambiguity, and self-confidence, relate positively and consistently to measures of creative performance across a variety of domains (Barron & Harrington, 1981; Cough, 1979; Martingales, 1989).

A number of questionnaire measures *have been developed* that attempt to reliably assess these personal characteristics. One of the most widely used and respected of these measures is Gough's Creative Personality Scale (CPS; Gough, 1979; Hocevar & Bachelor, 1989; Kaduson & Schaefer, 1991; McCrae, 1987). The CPS includes

...

As can be seen from these examples, the real purpose of the present perfect is to summarise the state of knowledge that has been established as the result of many studies, usually by a number of researchers. This opening summary is usually followed by examples of individual studies in that area and, as we can see from the examples above, the reporting verbs at that point can be in the simple present (*Lau's paper points out* ... in Example 2.31) or the simple past (*Herrington's profile* ... *illustrated* ... in Example 2.32).

Indicating the currently accepted state of affairs

In none of the above examples is the present perfect used to refer to only one researcher or one study. On the few occasions when it is used in this way, as is shown in Example 2.34 below, it is to indicate that the currently accepted state of affairs is different from what was previously accepted.

EXAMPLE 2.34

> Park's (1995) study *found* that consumption of only two units of alcohol could cause palpitations in women using the medication. This finding was confirmed by Truman's (1996) study. However, Billings (1996) *has found* that palpitations only occurred when the alcohol was consumed at the same time as the medication was taken.

In this example, even though the neutral verb 'to find' is used for Billings' study, rather than a stronger verb, such as 'demonstrated' or 'showed', the use of the present perfect in contrast to the past simple for Park's study indicates that Billings' findings are now taken to be correct and have superseded the findings of the other researchers.

TASK 2.4

In the following two texts all the verbs reporting on the literature have been removed. The infinitives for the verbs are listed below the text in random order. Place the correct verb, in the correct tense, in each of the numbered spaces.

Text 1

Several studies _____(1)_____ that bicarbonate is one of the salivary components that potentially modifies the formation of caries by changing the environmental pH and possibly the virulence of the bacteria that cause decay (Luoma and Luoma, 1967, 1968; Goldberg and Enslein, 1979; Luoma et al., 1979; Igarashi et al., 1988; Tanzer, 1989; Tanzer et al., 1987, 1988, 1990; Goldberg et al., 1990). In three different animal studies, Tanzer et al. (1987, 1988, 1990) _____(2)_____ the efficacy of a sodium bicarbonate based dental powder and paste with the addition of fluoride on dental caries and on Streptococcus sobrinus or Streptococcus mutans recoveries in rats. These authors _____(3)_____ that in rats exposed to the bicarbonate-based dentifrices, the recovery of S. sobrinus was 51–75% and that of S. mutans 34% lower when compared with the demineralized water controls. Further, the caries reductions in these studies ranged from 42 to 50% in the rats treated with bicarbonate dentifrices when compared with rats treated with water. It _____(4)_____ that bicarbonate exerted part of its anticaries effect by slowing the growth or altering the ecological advantage of S. sobrinus on the teeth and/or by a combination of anti-S. mutans and anti-'non-mutans' streptococci bacteriological effects. They also _____(5)_____ that caries inhibition may not be dependent on the buffering actions of bicarbonate against plaque acid, but more likely was the result of inhibition of enamel solubility and of augmentation of remineralization of enamel by the sodium bicarbonate.

Verb list

to test	to observe	to conclude
to suggest	to show	

Text 2

Previous research _____(6)_____ that complex jobs can have a positive and substantial impact on a variety of work-related outcomes (Cotton, 1993; Fried & Ferris, 1987; Kopelman, 1985). For example, numerous field studies _____(7)_____ measures of the five job characteristics identified in the previous paragraph and _____(8)_____ that an overall index of these characteristics, the Motivating Potential Score (MPS; Hackman & Oldham, 1980), explains substantial amounts of variance in measures of internal motivation (the extent to which employees experience positive feelings when they perform well and negative feelings when they perform poorly), job satisfaction, and overall performance (Fried &

Ferris, 1987). In addition, a few studies, _____(9)_____ some support for the link between the complexity of employees' jobs and their creative responses at work. Hatcher, Ross, and Collins (1989) _____(10)_____ a job complexity index by averaging employee reports of three job characteristics: autonomy, variety, and feedback. Their results _____(11)_____ positive, significant relations between this index and the number of new ideas employees submitted to an organization suggestion program. And a study by Amabile and Gryskiewicz (1989) _____(12)_____ significant relations between employee self-reports of creativity and of "freedom" and "challenging work".

Verb list

to create	to suggest	to provide
to rely on	to show	to demonstrate (used twice)

Criticising Others

Hedging

As noted earlier (**see 'Reasons for Referring', pp. 37–41**), when reviewing the literature in your field and working towards establishing a research space for your work, you may find it necessary to criticise some of the work that has already been done. Criticism is accepted in academic discourse, but you need to be aware of how to criticise tactfully in order to avoid giving offence. This is generally done by 'hedging' your criticisms, that is, by using certain words and expressions which tone down the criticism you are making. Hedged criticisms are illustrated in the examples below; the hedging words are italicised. (The topic of hedging will be discussed in more detail in Chapter 3 as the same type of language is commonly used when making claims about your own research findings.)

EXAMPLE 2.35

> Bachman (1990) gives a number of examples to illustrate situational
> authenticity including that of a reading test which reflects the topic
> and genre a student is likely to encounter outside a test situation
> and a test for copy typists. He claims that both are, in terms of
> situational authenticity, highly authentic. But these examples *appear*
> to have been rated on criteria no different to those used in the past.

EXAMPLE 2.36

> The authors do not give the details of their analysis, so it is not
> possible to quote examples, but it *seems* that they were interpreting
> the term 'cohesive tie' very loosely.

The use of these hedging verbs, 'appear' and 'seem', which make a
statement more tentative, softens the criticism by allowing for the
possibility that you, the writer of the criticism, have interpreted the other
person's research incorrectly. If we compare Examples 2.35 and 2.36
with Examples 2.35.1 and 2.36.1 below, where the hedging verbs have
been omitted, we can see that the criticism becomes much stronger
because it is written as though there is no doubt at all that the original
researcher was wrong.

EXAMPLE 2.35.1

> Bachman (1990) gives a number of examples to illustrate situational
> authenticity including that of a reading test which reflects the topic
> and genre a student is likely to encounter outside a test situation
> and a test for copy typists. He claims that both are, in terms of
> situational authenticity, highly authentic. But these examples have
> been rated on criteria no different to those used in the past.

EXAMPLE 2.36.1

> The authors do not give the details of their analysis, so it is not
> possible to quote examples, but they were interpreting the term
> 'cohesive tie' very loosely.

Balancing the negative points

Another common way of softening criticism is to preface the criticism with a balancing positive evaluation of the other person's work In Examples 2.37 and 2.38 below, the work of the researcher who is criticised, or at least some aspect of that researcher's work, is first of all praised, before the criticism is introduced.

EXAMPLE 2.37

> *Although the argument put forward by Alderson holds in that there is infinite variability of language which simulations can draw upon,* it does not acknowledge the consequences of using simulations, which *may be* far from trivial.

EXAMPLE 2.38

> *Despite Green's (1979) undoubtedly valuable contribution to the establishment of the criteria for assessing severe clinical depression,* her later research *tended* to be based on rather anecdotal "evidence"

In these examples we should notice that the actual criticism is, once again, hedged; the writers use *'may be'* and *'tended to be'* rather than the more certain *'is'*, so that there is, in effect, a double softener!

TASK 2.5

The following extract has been taken from a postgraduate dissertation in dentistry. Decide which part of the dissertation it most likely comes from. Then identify the hedges in the passage and decide how the language has been used to tone down the criticisms being made.

The studies mentioned above tried to compare the efficacy of Elyzol dental gel with subgingival scaling. It seems that the results of these studies gave a false image that Elyzol dental gel can be used in the initial therapy or to replace the subgingival scaling. As the gel is an antibiotic, it is reasonable that the gel should be applied only if the mechanical treatment fails to solve the pocket. Moreover, the study groups in the studies seem to have been poorly defined. In order to define the subject group better, subjects should perhaps be periodontally untreated patients, non-surgically treated patients or surgically treated patients.

Recently, a clinical and microbiological study of metronidazole 25% dental gel on recall subjects was reported (Stelzel & Flories-de-Jacoby, 1996). This was a randomised study with a slit-mouth design involving 30 recall patients. Metronidazole 25% dental gel treatment was compared with subgingival scaling. Clinical results showed no statistically significant differences between the two treatment modalities. Mean reduction in the probing pocket depth was 1.3 min after metronidazole 25% dental gel and 1.5 min after subgingival scaling and the results were very similar to those studies on previously untreated patients. In addition, the microbiological results have shown that both treatments yielded a post-treatment microflora comparable with health. In this study, the subjects were better defined. They were periodontally treated patients under a recall programme. However, it should be noted that smokers were included in the analysis of data which may have affected the results in this study.

Bringing It All Together

Reasons for referring

There are five primary reasons for referring to the work of other researchers:

❖ to acknowledge the work and ideas of others in order not to be accused of plagiarism;

❖ to demonstrate familiarity with the field in order to establish your membership of a particular academic community;

❖ to evaluate/analyse other researchers by showing your support for another researcher's work or refuting someone else's claims about his/her findings;

❖ to add support to your own findings and thereby give more authority to your statements;

❖ to create a research space by showing what has already been done and what has not been done in your area.

You need to think carefully about the reasons you have for making a reference as this will help you to decide on the language that you should use in each situation.

Methods of referring

There are five common methods of citation used in academic texts. You may:

❖ place the name of the researcher(s) in brackets after the reference;

❖ use a bracketed number after the reference;

❖ use a superscript after the reference;

❖ use 'according to' before the name of the researcher(s);

❖ grammatically integrate the name of the researcher(s) into the sentence as the subject.

Integrated citations, which are more common in dissertations than journal articles, allow you to give more information about your evaluation of the research reviewed and, therefore, make your stance towards the research clearer.

Language for Referring

Choice of verbs

Your reporting verb can show:
- ❖ your attitude to the research being reported;
- ❖ the original researcher's attitude to his/her own research.

Adjectives and adverbs

When using adjectives and adverbs to show your opinion of the research being reported on:
- ❖ they should be used sparingly;
- ❖ emotion-laden or colloquial terms should be avoided.

Verb tense

When deciding on the tense:
- ❖ the past simple must be used to refer to what was done in a single completed study or series of studies;
- ❖ both past and present simple can be used when what was written in a paper, rather than what was done, is being referred to;
- ❖ the present simple is generally used to indicate the currency of a debate;
- ❖ the present perfect is used to refer to a whole area of study before individual examples of studies in that area are described in the past or present simple;
- ❖ the present perfect indicates that the currently accepted state of affairs is different from what was previously accepted.

Criticising others

When you criticise other researchers, you need to be tactful about this. In order to soften your criticism, you may:
- ❖ use hedging words;
- ❖ point to positive features of the research before you criticise.

Use of Sources in Academic Papers

The reasons for referring to sources are generally the same in academic papers as in dissertations, except there is less need and less room to demonstrate familiarity with the field to establish your membership of an academic community. Choice of verbs and tense are equally important in both types of writing. However, evaluations of other researchers, particularly criticisms, are probably made with greater caution in academic papers than in dissertations. This is partly because journal articles reach a wider audience and there is, therefore, greater scope for creating offence and also because a paper with heavy criticism will not pass a peer review!

Another rather noticeable difference between journal articles and dissertations, particularly in science and engineering disciplines, is that in articles there tend to be fewer integrated citations, where the researcher is the subject of the sentence; superscripts are commonly used or the researchers are mentioned only in brackets at the end of the sentence. This is most likely because journal articles tend to describe, rather than evaluate other research and, therefore, integrated references are not so essential.

Further Advice

Disciplines vary considerably in the verbs, adjectives and adverbs that they prefer to use in academic writing and in the frequency with which they use different techniques of citation. You should try as much as possible to fit in with the conventions.

Pay attention also to the use of footnotes and endnotes, which are far more common in some disciplines than others. Consider why the information in a footnote has been placed there rather than in the body of the text.

Follow-up Tasks

1. As you are reading through papers in your own discipline, check which words are most commonly used to show the different attitudes the writer takes towards the research being reported. Keep a list of these for use in your own writing. Note also whether writers generally use the present or past simple to refer to what has been written or said by other researchers, as opposed to what has been done.

2. Look at how writers most often make references in your discipline. Note when and where they use the name of the researcher as the subject of the sentence as opposed to using a superscript or placing the name in brackets at the end of the sentence. Consider why the writers have chosen to use each particular method.

3. Take one aspect of your research and write a review of the literature relating to the area you have selected. Decide how you will refer to the sources in advance and make sure you adhere to the method selected (i.e. alphabetical/numerical).

3 Stating Facts, Interpreting Data and Making Claims

Although the organisation of your dissertation will depend largely on the type of research you are conducting, the rhetorical moves you will need to make and the language you use to make them will generally be very similar across disciplines. In all dissertations you will need to state facts, interpret data and make claims. This chapter focuses on how this is done.

Typically, in experimental research the methods and results sections of the dissertation are associated with the statement of facts. In the methods section you tell your readers what you did and how you did it, while in the results section you tell them what you found. It is only after you have provided this information that you can move on to account for your findings and suggest what the implications of those findings may be. The subsequent discussion, therefore, moves from statements of fact, about which there can be no argument, to your interpretations, which will always be subject to dispute/disagreement.

In non-experimental research it is unlikely that you will have separate methods, results and discussion sections/chapters, but you will still need to make the same moves from fact to interpretation. If, for example, your research aims to investigate 'The development of the film industry in the West since the tragedy of September 11th', you will first have to inform your readers about the events of 11 September 2001 and of the relevant developments in the film industry subsequent to the tragedy. These statements of fact will be followed by any conclusions you draw about the relationship between the two; the conclusions are your interpretations only and you will need to make that clear to your readers through the language you use.

Understanding how we distinguish fact from interpretation is very important, particularly at this level of writing. In the task that follows we look at how this is achieved.

TASK 3.1

Look at the following statements, some of which have been extracted from the results section and some from the discussion section of a medical journal article on skin cancer in children. Decide which statements come from which section and think about how the language used is different in the two sections.

1. Our finding of a low melanocytic naevi in redheads is unlikely to be due to small sample size ...
2. Children who have been sunburnt were twice as likely as children who had never been sunburnt to have very high numbers of melanocytic naevi ...
3. If the relation between melanocytic naevi frequency and melanoma risk is the same for children as for adults, then the pattern of risk seems to be established very early in life in Queensland children in the tropics.
4. Children who averaged more than 4 hours per day in the sun were three times as likely to have high numbers of melanocytic naevi than were children who spent 1 hour or less per day ...
5. It seems that living in Townsville is, in itself, sufficient for children to acquire large numbers of melanocytic naevi early in life ...
6. Children who had at least one episode of sunburn had more than twice as many melanocytic naevi compared with children who had never been sunburnt.
7. Melanocytic naevi also increased with the total number of hours spent in the sun in the year before examination ...

8. Our results suggest that this may be explained by sun-avoidance in the most sunsensitive group ...

9. Significantly more melanocytic naevi were associated with light neutral skin colour compared with other skin types ... and with darker hair colour – 28 for red/auburn hair, 30.5 for blonde/fair hair, and 43 for dark hair (p=0.0001).

STATING FACTS

The following statements from Task 3.1 above are from the results section of the article.

2. Children who have been sunburnt were twice as likely as children who had never been sunburnt to have very high numbers of melanocytic naevi ...

4. Children who averaged more than 4 hours per day in the sun were three times as likely to have high numbers of melanocytic naevi than were children who spent 1 hour or less per day ...

6. Children who had at least one episode of sunburn had more than twice as many melanocytic naevi compared with children who had never been sunburnt.

7. Melanocytic naevi also increased with the total number of hours spent in the sun in the year before examination ...

9. Significantly more melanocytic naevi were associated with light neutral skin colour compared with other skin types ... and with darker hair colour – 28 for red/auburn hair, 30.5 for blonde/fair hair, and 43 for dark hair (p=0.0001).

We know this because they state facts, i.e. they convey information that is not open to argument. It is the function of the results or findings section/chapter to report the facts that have been uncovered during the research, just as it is the function of the methods section/chapter to report the facts on how the research was conducted. The following examples further illustrate writing from the methods and results sections of journals and dissertations. Example 3.1 is extracted from a paper in a linguistics journal and Example 3.2 from a paper in a physics journal.

EXAMPLE 3.1

A pre-test was administered and informal conversations followed each of the pre-test sessions. Ten subjects were then selected. Three native English speakers, all Cambridge University students, were used for checking the suitability of the test for the study.

EXAMPLE 3.2

The n-GaN films used in this study were epitaxially grown by hydride vapour phase epitaxy on (0001) sapphire substrates. The thickness of the active layer was 20µm. The nominal carrier concentration, deduced from Hall measurements, was 1.5×10^{17} cm^{-3}, and the electron mobility was $600cm^2V^{-1}_s{}^{1}$. The GaN films were cleaned in organic solvents, etched in 1:1 HCl:DI water, rinsed in DI water and dried in N_2 gas. The samples were immediately transferred to a vacuum chamber for the deposition of ohmic contacts. ...

Example 3.3 is from the *results* section of a health care journal, while Example 3.4 is from the *findings* section of a paper in a surgery journal.

EXAMPLE 3.3

Overall locus of controlled scores was higher in the homebound sample (p=.001). Further analysis of the locus of control-rating scale scores showed homebound persons' internal beliefs in expected control to be higher than those of nursing home residents (p=.001) and that there was a similar trend noted (p=0.086) between groups in desired control. Both samples showed differences within each group between desired and expected control (see Table 2). There was no difference in life satisfaction scores between the two groups.

EXAMPLE 3.4

> In group A, the 3 patients had no detectable immunoglobulins, C3, or fibrin within the granulomas. In group B, fluorescent antisera did detect trace amounts if IgG and C3 complement associated with large quantities of fibrin in the capsule of one clinically intact prosthesis. The contralateral capsule on this patient stained for fibrin but not for immunoglobulins or C3 complement. One other capsule biopsy stained positive for fibrin. Gel droplets surrounded by a foreign-body response were seen in most of the capsular biopsies in group B. In group C biopsies, all antisera studies were negative except for one specimen positive for C3. The amount of gel in the capsules was generally greater in this group. The foreign-body response was more intense and proportional to the amount of gel present.

STATING FACTS: LANGUAGE FEATURES

Describing Actions

Tense

It is important to note that when reporting on what you did or what you found in your studies or experiments, it is most common to use the **simple past tense** as the examples above show. Remember that there is no difference between describing what you did in your research and describing what you did on your holidays last year; you are describing actions which are completed at the time of writing.

This choice of tense allows you, the writer, to easily distinguish between what you did and the standard procedure that is generally used when this type of study is conducted. It may be especially important for you to stress this if you altered some part of the procedure. If we change the text in Example 3.2 above into the **simple present tense** (as shown in 3.2.2 below), then it would change from being a description of what was done in a particular study to a description of what is usually done as a matter of course when carrying out such studies.

Example 3.2.1	Example 3.2.2
The n-GaN films used in this study *were* epitaxially *grown* by hydride vapour phase epitaxy on (0001) sapphire substrates. The thickness of the active layer *was* 20µm. The nominal carrier concentration, deduced from Hall measurements, *was* 1.5 x 10^{17} cm^{-3}, and the electron mobility *was* 600cm^{2}V$^{-1}_s$^{1}. The GaN films *were cleaned* in organic solvents, *etched* in 1:1 HCl:DI water, *rinsed* in DI water and *dried* in N$_2$ gas. The samples *were* immediately *transferred* to a vacuum chamber for the deposition of ohmic contacts. ...	The n-GaN films used *are* epitaxially *grown* by hydride vapour phase epitaxy on (0001) sapphire substrates. The thickness of the active layer *is* 20µm. The nominal carrier concentration, deduced from Hall measurements, *is* 1.5 x 10^{17} cm^{-3}, and the electron mobility *is* 600cm^{2}V$^{-1}_s$^{1}. The GaN films *are cleaned* in organic solvents, *etched* in 1:1 HCl:DI water, *rinsed* in DI water and *dried* in N$_2$ gas. The samples *are* immediately *transferred* to a vacuum chamber for the deposition of ohmic contacts. ...

Note:

In some disciplines it may be the convention, where the standard procedure was the one used in that particular research, to specifically note this before describing that procedure in the **past simple**, as in Example 3.5.

EXAMPLE 3.5

The standard procedure was used in my research. ES cells (10–15) with mutated CollOa-1 allele were injected into the blastocel cavities of C57BL/6J blastocysts at 3.5 days post coitum. After injection, the blastocysts were then surgically transferred to the uteri of pseudopregnant recipient mice at 2.5 days post coitum. Pups were born 17 days after transfer and identified visually as chimeric on the basis of coat colour.

Voice

Notice that the verbs which have been italicised in the extracts below are all in the passive voice. This is generally the practice when writing the methods section/chapter and is quite common when reporting the results.

EXAMPLE 3.6

A pre-test *was administered* and informal conversations followed each of the pre-test sessions. Ten subjects *were* then *selected*. Three native English speakers, all Cambridge University students, were used for checking the suitability of the test for the study.

EXAMPLE 3.7

The GaN films *were cleaned* in organic solvents, *etched* in 1:1 HCI:DI water, *rinsed* in DI water and *dried* in N_2 gas. The samples *were* immediately *transferred* to a vacuum chamber for the deposition of ohmic contacts. ...

In Chapter 1 we pointed out that the use of 'I' is acceptable nowadays, but the first person pronoun should not be overused. It would be very annoying for the reader if all the sentences in this section of your dissertation started with 'I', and using the passive voice here allows you to avoid such a problem.

Referring to Tables and Figures

Verb tense

It is common in the results section to present tables and figures to illustrate the findings. When referring to these tables and figures you are no longer reporting on what you found, but reporting on what can be seen in the piece of writing which the reader is looking at. For this reason, the **simple present tense,** either active or passive as appropriate, is generally used, as can be seen in the statements given in Example 3.8.

EXAMPLE 3.8

1. Based on this logic, *Table 2 shows* the findings of the three models.
2. The following *two tables* (Tables 5.1 & 5.2) *show* the minimum,

maximum and mean length of interactions, range, and standard deviation for each group.

3.   *In Fig. 7* a small deviation between the measured data and the calculated curve *is seen* for large values of B_z.

4.   The areas of the 34 'grasses' were able to be estimated in this way, and the results *are presented in Table 2* within the six size classes.

Sentence construction

It is not possible in English to refer to a figure or table in the following ways:

(a) In Figure 3, it shows ...   **(X)**
(b) From Table 5, it illustrates ...   **(X)**

Very occasionally in conversational English it may be possible to follow a noun immediately by a pronoun referring to that noun, but in formal, written English this is grammatically incorrect. If you begin an opening phrase with a preposition, you can either use the passive in the following clause, as in Example 3.9 below, or you can begin the clause with a personal pronoun, as in Example 3.10.

EXAMPLE 3.9

In Figure 3, it can be seen that ...

EXAMPLE 3.10

From Table 5, we can observe that ...

It is much more straightforward, however, to omit the preposition and the pronoun as in Example 3.11.

EXAMPLE 3.11

Figure 3 shows ...
Table 5 illustrates ...

INTERPRETING DATA AND MAKING CLAIMS

Separating Facts and Claims

We now turn to look more closely at ways in which researchers put forward their own interpretations of the data from their research and make claims about their findings. If we look back at Task 3.1, we can see that the following statements 1, 3, 5, and 8 were all taken from the discussion section of the paper on melanocytic naevi.

1. Our finding of a low melanocytic naevi in redheads is unlikely to be due to small sample size …

3. If the relation between melanocytic naevi frequency and melanoma risk is the same for children as for adults, then the pattern of risk seems to be established very early in life in Queensland children in the tropics.

5. It seems that living in Townsville is, in itself, sufficient for children to acquire large numbers of melanocytic naevi early in life …

8. Our results suggest that this may be explained by sun-avoidance in the most sunsensitive group …

We can tell this because these statements are not stating facts, they are telling readers how the researchers believe their findings can be interpreted; that is, they are making claims about their own findings. It is always possible that other researchers could give a different interpretation and this is why all these statements are tentative. The claims made are 'hedged'; in other words, the writers have limited the claims they make by using certain words that make the claims more tentative. These words and phrases are the same ones that are used to hedge criticisms of other researchers as discussed in Chapter 2. The use of these words is one way that a writer has of showing that s/he is not stating a fact, but making an interpretation.

Reasons for Hedging

There are two reasons why you need to hedge some of the claims you make when writing up your research.

1. You need to be **modest**. The studies or experiments that you have conducted may not provide a definitive answer to the questions you posed or be the only explanation for the findings you have noted. If you do not show some modesty, you will sound arrogant and are in danger of annoying your readers. In being modest, you acknowledge that your findings are only a point along the way to greater knowledge and that you cannot give the same weight to the interpretation of your data as you can to established facts.

2. You need to be **cautious** to avoid the embarrassment of being proved wrong after making claims that are too strong. Being cautious will also help protect your reputation and that of your supervisor. If later studies, based on new findings or technological advances, show that your interpretation was not, in fact, the correct one, you will look quite foolish if you have stated, categorically, that yours was the definitive answer.

INTERPRETING DATA AND MAKING CLAIMS: LANGUAGE FEATURES

Hedging Devices

The sentences from Task 3.1 are repeated in Column 1 of Table 3.1 on p. 79 and the hedging devices are italicised. In comparison, the statements in Column 2 are not hedged; they have been rewritten, without the hedging devices, to sound as though the researchers are stating facts, the truth of which is indisputable. Think about the impact each version has on the reader.

Table 3.1   Hedging illustrated

Column 1	Column 2
Our finding of a low melanocytic naevi in redheads *is unlikely* to be due to small sample size ...	Our finding of a low melanocytic naevi in redheads *is not* due to small sample size ...
If the relation between melanocytic naevi frequency and melanoma risk is the same for children as for adults, then the pattern of risk *seems to be established* very early in life in Queensland children in the tropics.	If the relation between melanocytic naevi frequency and melanoma risk is the same for children as for adults, then the pattern of risk *is established* very early in life in Queensland children in the tropics.
It *seems* that living in Townsville is, in itself, sufficient for children to acquire large numbers of melanocytic naevi early in life...	Living in Townsville *is*, in itself, sufficient for children to acquire large numbers of melanocytic naevi early in life...
Our results *suggest* that this *may* be explained by sun-avoidance in the most sunsensitive group ...	Our results *show* that this *is* explained by sun-avoidance in the most sunsensitive group ...

The examples below further illustrate the use of tentative language. Example 3.12 is from a paper published in a history journal and Example 3.13 is from one in a journal of anthropology.

EXAMPLE 3.12

This begs the major question about African perception of white people and colonial authority in Africa before the war. Certainly the strikes, riots and 'hold-ups' of the nineteen-thirties *do not indicate* that Africans invested whites with god-like status. Despite Sithole's argument, it is *probable* that views about white prestige emanated mainly from white people themselves!

Many historians since the nineteen-sixties have stressed the important role of ex-servicemen in post-war nationalist politics, but the evidence for this is thin. Recent research presents a different view – that ex-soldiers were no more significant in territorial politics than any other occupational group. The idea that men from the bush *might* sit in Bombay bars discussing with Indian nationalists the overthrow of colonial rule *seems* far-fetched. The rare soldier's letter arguing for political change and intercepted by the censor, needs to be placed alongside the hundreds of letters which express the real concerns of soldiers away from home – family, land, crops, cattle and prospects after demobilization. Certainly such domestic and social concerns *could be* translated into political demands, but they rarely were. Most African soldiers returned to their rural homes, where some exercised a significant political role challenging the authority of chiefs and questioning accepted ideas and practices. Unfortunately relatively little research was done on grassroots rural politics in the late nineteen-forties and early nineteen-fifties and now it *may be* too late to recapture that interesting and significant aspect of African history.

EXAMPLE 3.13

The results of Hawkes (2001) study among hunter gathers *suggest* that male hunters *generally* share their meat among the whole group rather than reserving it for mates and offspring. Hawkes believes that this behaviour *probably* adds to their prestige and thus increases the number of mates they acquire as the females *tend* to be attracted to those men who are seen to be good providers. In similar vein, Weissner's (2002), study of foragers in Botswana and New Guinea *indicates* that the sharing out of meat is intended to be influential in the political arena, as those who have been regularly provided with meat by a hunter will feel an obligation to follow or support that man in any leadership challenge.

Hrdy (2003) notes that these findings *appear* to cast doubt on the presumptions made by earlier researchers that fathers hunted to provide for their own offspring only and that, for this reason, a woman would mate with only one man so that the paternity of her children was not in question and these children would, therefore, be provided for. This idea does not take into account that a hunter *may not return* with a good catch for his children and, indeed, *may not return* at all, death on hunting trips being far from uncommon. In these circumstances, relying on one mate as a provider of food would be distinctly disadvantageous to a woman. Hrdy's (2002) studies amongst the Canela and Ache tribes of the Amazon *suggest* that the "one-man" woman is not the norm in hunter gather society. Women *often* have multiple partners as each man who has had sex with a woman in the 10 months or so before she gives birth is considered to be a possible father and is, therefore, responsible for the upkeep of that child. This practice, of what Hrdy (2003) refers to as "polyandrous motherhood", *seems to be* a deliberate strategy on the part of the women of the tribes to ensure support for any children they bear. Other tribes in the region, for example the Bari and the Yanamamo, hold the belief that a foetus is created by a build up of semen from different men (Hill, 2002), *implying* that a child *could be* supported by many fathers.

TASK 3.2

There are a number of ways in which claims can be made more tentative. Table 3.2 on p. 82 summarises the range of linguistic devices commonly used to hedge claims. Complete the table with further examples from this chapter or ones you identify in your own reading. Try to identify at least three examples for each category.

Table 3.2 Hedging devices

Device	Example	
Hedging verbs	indicate	Feedback from this group at the end of the task *indicated* that although they had not had enough time to complete the task ... (Example 3.3)
Adverbs	probably	... the degradation of benzoate into acetate was *probably* conducted completely inside the cell ... (Example 3.14)
Adjectives	likely/unlikely	Our findings of a low melanocytic naevi in redheads is *unlikely* to be due to small sample size (Task 3.1)
Modal verbs	may	Our results suggest that this *may* be explained by sun-avoidance in the most sunsensitive group (Task 3.1)
Modal nouns	probability	There appears to be a strong *probability* that the students' use of English discourse patterns reflects the fact that Arabic discourse patterns do not differ radically from English ones ... (Example 3.15)
Reference to model/theory	if (this theory is correct), then ...	*If* the relation between melanocytic naevi frequency and melanoma risk is the same for children as for adults, *then* ... (Task 3.1)

Combining Facts and Claims

It is important to note that the discussion is not always a separate section of a dissertation or journal article. Many writers combine the results and discussion into a single section/chapter as in Example 3.14 below, taken from an MPhil in civil engineering, where the writer first states one result, then discusses it before moving on to the next result and its discussion. In this case, the language for stating facts and that for interpreting data will alternate. How you present your results and discussion will largely depend on the complexity of your results and whether you need to draw on several different results in your discussion. If your results are complex, it is advisable to state all your results first and then discuss them. This type of organisation is easier, but some writers feel it leads to too much repetition.

EXAMPLE 3.14

Results and Discussion

Table 4 summarises the SMA data of the phenol-degrading granules using six individual substrates, including formate, acetate, propionate, butyrate, benzoate and phenol. The phenol-degrading granules were found capable of degrading benzoate. Using benzoate as the sole substrate, the granules had an SMA of 0.244 g-COD/g-VSS/day which was comparable to the 0.23 g-CODg-VSS/day using phenol as the sole substrate. This *seems to support* Kobyashi's (1989) pathway that phenol was degraded by first converting to benzoate. This was further confirmed by the presence in large quantities of Syntrophus buswellii-like bacteria in the granules, as to be discussed in the next section.

Table 4.3 also shows that the granules' SMS using either phenol or benzoate as substrates were significantly less than those using formate (0.98 g-COD/g-VSS/day) and acetate (0.64 g-COD/g-VSS/day) as substrates. This *seems to suggest* that the initial conversion from phenol/benzoate to VFAs was *likely to be* the rate-limiting step in the anaerobic degradation of phenol. In addition, the phenol-degradation granules did not exhibit any methanogenic activity when propionate and butyrate were used as substrate. This further *suggests* that the degradation of benzoate into acetate was *probably* conducted completely inside the cell of the Syntrophus buswellii-like bacteria; acetate was then released to the mixed liquor to be degraded by acetrophic methanogens. Such a postulation was supported by the observation that there was no detectable propionate and butyrate in the effluent.

Making Claims throughout the Dissertation

In the humanities, where there are often no separate sections/chapters for findings and discussion, tentative propositions occur at various stages as the writer wishes to present an interpretation of the facts observed. However, often such statements appear towards the end of a section or chapter. Example 3.15 below appears close to the end of Chapter 3 of an MPhil dissertation in applied linguistics, where the author is discussing the results of one part of the investigation carried out in the research. Example 3.16 comes from the end of a section in a journal article on contemporary Chinese culture.

Example 3.15

This would *seem to suggest* that knowledge of another European language did not prevent first language features from being carried over into English. If students did not transfer punctuation and stylistic features from French into English, there *seem to be* no grounds for assuming that they transferred discourse patterns from French. There *appears to be a strong probability* that the students' use of English discourse patterns reflects the fact that Arabic discourse patterns do not differ radically from English ones, at least in so far as expository texts are concerned. Written discourse *may differ* in the style of presentation between the two cultures, but the style merely reflects superficial syntactic differences, not contrasting methods of overall discourse structure.

Example 3.16

The former couple's musings seem to have been *interrupted* by the arrival of the food. This *may suggest* that their conflicts and divorce were caused by daily trivialities. However, the heroine's musings *may* also *symbolize* the peace of mind she finally obtains: although she still in some sense remains emotionally attached to him, she is able to regard their separation as a renewal, or even as the rebirth of her female subjectivity. Indeed, this is where she becomes creative and is able to face him and present herself confidently and calmly for the first time. Her rebirth is based on an escape from the "prison" of marriage and a refusal to serve as a "mirrored" image for the male subject.

"On the Same Horizon" is regarded as a piece of autobiographical fiction. There is a mirroring or doubling effect in the relationship both between the female I-narrator and the story, and between the author and her story. Zhang Xinxin was in fact facing a marriage crisis when she wrote the novella. The repeated self-doubting questions of the heroine *may have been* the very questions that beset Zhang Xinxin herself: "What can be done?", "Is it finished like this?", "What's wrong?", and "Family, husband … can I really shoulder all the wifely duties any longer?".

TASK 3.3

Read through the following paragraph, which has been extracted from a section of a paper in a business journal entitled, *Discussion and Conclusion*. It does not include any tentative language. Given that the extract discusses the findings from a single study, how would you rewrite it to make the authors' claims sound less certain, more tentative?

Discussion and Conclusion

This article endeavors to make some progress in those directions. It shows that both property- and knowledge-based resources that are hard to buy or imitate contributed to performance returns on sales, operating profits, and market share. However, the environmental context was all-important in conditioning these relationships. Periods of stability and predictability favored firms with property-based resources but did not reward those with knowledge-based resources. Precisely the opposite was true for periods of uncertainty, even though the sample of firms was identical. It follows then, that whether or not an asset can be considered a resource will depend as much on the context enveloping an organization as on the properties of the asset itself. It is misleading to attempt to define resources independent of the tasks they are to serve and the environment within which they must function (cf. Barney, 1991).

Acknowledging Limitations

Another means by which you can make your claims more tentative is by acknowledging the limitations of your study. By doing this you are, in effect, toning down the claims you are making, i.e. hedging, and showing there is room for further research. Example 3.17 below, taken from a sociology journal, shows how to acknowledge limitations. The numbers in brackets indicate the sentence number for ease of reference.

Example 3.17

Limitations

Several limitations of the study are worth noting. [1] The study employed a convenience, non-random sample, which could have resulted in a selection bias, and thus influenced the results. [2] The small sample size, which limited the number of variables that could be included in the regression analysis, also limits the generalizability of the findings and weakened the statistical power of the analysis. [3] Certain variables pertinent to Pearlin et al.'s (1990) model were not included in the original study and thus could not be examined. [4] The effects of these omissions are not known. [5] As mentioned above, the use of a two-item coping scale, which only assessed the presence of informal support, did not allow for a more comprehensive testing of this complex construct. [6] Furthermore, since the initial intake did not include objective diagnostic verification, there was no way of confirming that the patient's symptoms were dementia-related at the time of intake. [7] Although, subsequent referrals for diagnostic verification by a health care provider have correlated highly with the caregiver's report of symptoms, level of impairment, etc. (Rosa Ramirez, personal communication, Sept. 2, 1999). [8] Finally, although the majority were of Mexican American descent, the study combined several subgroups of Latinos. [9] Therefore, the findings may not be generalizable to Latinos from other subgroups. [10] Despite these limitations, the findings offer direction for future areas of inquiry, especially in light of the paucity of research on the Latino caregiving experience. [11]

The limitations noted in the text are (numbers in brackets refer to the sentence within the text):

1. the non-random nature of the sample [2]
2. the small size of the sample [3]
3. omitted variables [4]
4. use of a two-item scale [6]
5. lack of objective diagnostic verification [7]
6. poorly defined groups [9]

We should note, however, that the writer does not only identify the limitations of the study, but points out either how the limitation may have affected the results or acknowledges that the effect of the limitation is not known:

(a) Limitation 1

... which could have resulted in a selection bias [2]

(b) Limitation 2

... which limited the number of variables that could be included in the regression analysis, also limits the generalizability of the findings and weakened the statistical power of the analysis [3]

(c) Limitation 3

The effects of these omissions are not known [5]

(d) Limitation 4

... did not allow for a more comprehensive testing of this complex construct [6]

(e) Limitation 5

... there was no way of confirming that the patient's symptoms were dementia-related at the time of intake [7]

(f) Limitation 6

... the findings may not be generalizable to Latinos from other subgroups [10]

By acknowledging the limitations and their possible effects on the findings, a writer hopes to help future researchers to avoid the same errors or suggests a better approach for future investigations.

TASK 3.4

Read through the following text, which is extracted from an article on educational psychology, and note down the limitations of the study that are acknowledged by the authors. Note also what possible effect each limitation might have had on the study.

Limitations of the Present Study

Several limitations of the present study should be noted. [1] First, whereas most homework research has been conducted in the United States, our sample consists of German students. [2] As noted earlier, the U.S. and German school systems differ, for instance, in that students in Germany are tracked, and students in the United States have more freedom in terms of which classes to take. [3] Although the average time spent on math homework is comparable in both student and teacher reports across the two countries (Beaton et al., 1996), there might be other, nontrivial differences. [4] For instance, there may be differences in the quality of the exercises assigned. [5] Therefore, the study would have been stronger had it included a cross-cultural comparison. [6]

It should also be emphasized that our results are restricted to mathematics. [7] Homework assignments may play a different role in other school subjects where homework has a different character (e.g., the acquisition of vocabulary in foreign language classes). [8] Therefore, the relation between typical homework length and achievement gains might be different in, for instance, foreign language classes. [9]

Moreover, our study is focused on 7th-grade students. [10] It should be noted that previous research suggested that homework effects are larger in higher grades and smaller (or nonexistent) in lower grades (e.g., Cooper, 1989). [11] Therefore, it would possibly be misleading to make inferences about other grades on the basis of our results. [12]

Previous research has also indicated that collecting, correcting, and grading of homework might strengthen the relationship between homework and achievement gains (Walberg et al., 1985). [13] This finding was not replicated in our study. [14] Our data, however, do not allow this aspect to be addressed in detail. [15] The variable used in our study, "homework monitoring," should be refined for use in further studies, as it encompasses too many meanings. [16] For instance, it could imply a short check of whether all students have completed their homework, it could mean integrating the results of the homework exercises into the next lesson, or it could involve collecting and correcting the homework assignments. [17] Video analyses of German mathematics lessons in grade 8 seem to indicate that homework monitoring is frequently restricted to a check on whether homework was completed (Neubrand, 2000). [18]

Nevertheless, the measure used in this study leaves room for different interpretations and might be responsible for the rather small correlation between homework monitoring and achievement gains. [19] We further note that homework frequency and homework monitoring were each measured by a single self-report item. [20] Moreover, the time variable used only a 3-point scale. [21]

Our study concentrated on variables that can be influenced by teachers. [22] Achievement gains, however, are also related to how students spend their leisure time (Cooper et al., 1999; Eccles & Barber, 1999; Keith, Reimers, Fehrmann, Pottebaum, & Aubey, 1986). [23] For instance, students who spend some of their free time solving mathematical problems might exhibit higher achievement. [24] Though it is important not to mix up homework and additional math-based activities in leisure time, further studies should include additional measures of such activities. [25]

Moreover, nonacademic outcomes were not considered in this study. [26] It should be noted that homework assignments have been ascribed both positive and negative effects on variables such as motivation, morale, and exhaustion (cf. Cooper, 1989; Cooper et al., 1998). [27]

Finally, the greatest danger of nonexperimental research is the exclusion of a common cause and supposed effect. [28] Although much care was taken to control for possible confounding variables and alternative explanations, randomized experimental trials could help to further clarify the effects found in our study. [29]

TASK 3.5

Read through the extracts below, taken from journal articles in ecology (Text 1), sociology (Text 2), and literature and language (Text 3), decide which part of the text the extract has been taken from and identify the hedges used by the writers.

Text 1

Our results suggested that culvert attributes influence species' use but different attributes appeared to affect use by different species. One common theme at all scales of resolution — individual species, species group and community level — was that traffic volume, and, to a lesser degree, noise levels and road width, ranked high as significant factors affecting species' use of culverts.

One would expect that as road width increased medium-sized forest mammals would be increasingly vulnerable. The risk of predation while attempting to cross exposed road corridors may be greater as well (Korpimaki & Norrdahl 1989; Rodriguez, Crema & Delibes, 1996). Coyotes, being the largest of the mammal species studied, tended to use culverts less in high traffic density situations, whereas three of the four smaller mammals (martens, snowshoe hares and red squirrels), and not surprisingly the three-species group, showed greater use of the passages. Forrest-associated mammal species generally avoid open areas without overstorey or shrub cover (Buskirk & Powell 1994; Ruggiero et al. 1994) and we would expect the same response to an open corridor (Oxley, Fenton & Carmody 1974; Mader 1984; Swihart & Slade 1984). Culvert use by these species might be a response to this fragmented and unsafe habitat and a result of learned behaviour passed on by surviving individuals selecting culverts for cross-highway travel.

Text 2

The findings of this study are confined to physical abuse. Although the detrimental effect of mental abuse on a relationship should not be ignored, only a small proportion of the women involved in this study complained of verbal or mental abuse.. The possibility that mental abuse, by lowering the women's self-esteem, may exacerbate the effects of the physical abuse cannot be rejected, but a separate study would be needed to ratify such a suggestion.

A further note of caution is necessary when generalizing from this sample. The vast majority of the women studied came from low income families where the husband had relatively little education and the results, therefore, may be a function of the sample. Other studies, however, have suggested that neither of these variables increases the possibility of violence in a relationship; similar patterns of violence have been found in homes across the social spectrum and at all educational levels.

Perhaps the major limitation of this study is the sample size. However, the consistency of the pattern of the development of violence suggests that the observations would hold true for a larger sample.

Text 3

As this brief walking tour through literary history indicates, "The Changing Light" draws equally from all kinds of literary tradition. The epic is promiscuous in the choice of its sources: like Seneca's bee, Merrill gathers the nectar of multiple poetic models and transforms it into the pure honey of his own magnum opus. Through his synthesis of autobiography and memory, through his free, indiscriminate, and seemingly haphazard borrowing from former literary works, the poet produces a controlled fantasy of becoming an equal with Homer, Dante, Spenser, Milton, Blake and Yeats. But putting Merrill in that notable company of literary masters only does injustice to his poetry as a whole; his remarks at Harvard were no doubt heartfelt, but also delicately sarcastic. Should we instead begin by trying to situate the trilogy in the tradition of the American long poem? *The Waste Land* seems a likely precursor, though we can only go so far in claiming Merrill's poetic affinity with Eliot. After the publication of the whole of *Sandover* in 1982, Merrill was promoted from customary inclusion in poetic anthologies to what at this point seems to be a permanent place in the history of twentieth-century American literature. ... In *The Western Canon* which came out more than a decade after *Sandover*, Harold Bloom regards Merrill as probably the most important American poet of the latter part of the twentieth century next to John Ashbery.

Bringing It All Together

Points to remember:

❖ It is important that you distinguish between facts and your interpretations of data throughout your dissertation.

❖ Statements of fact are prevalent throughout the methods and results sections of a dissertation.

❖ When making claims about your own research and when criticising the research of others you need to use tentative language, that is, you need to hedge what you say.

❖ There are numerous linguistic devices which you can use to hedge. You should familiarise yourself with those more commonly used within your field of study. As you read, you should make a note of the way experienced writers in your field hedge.

Hedging in Academic Papers

The use of hedging in academic papers is similar to that in dissertations. Many of the examples in this chapter have been taken from journal articles, precisely because of the similarity between the two types of writing. It is, however, important to remember that if you want to have a paper published in a refereed journal, you need to be especially careful to tone down your criticism of accomplished academics. Editors pay considerable attention to the ability to manipulate this type of language when making decisions about publishing a paper. This does not mean that you should not criticise other people's work — it simply means that you must show caution in the ways demonstrated in this chapter.

Follow-up Tasks

1   Identify two or three papers in your field and look at the way

the studies are written up. Do the papers have methods/results sections? How much tentative language can you find?

2. Take a paper in your field and write a paragraph or two critiquing it. When pointing out its strengths and weaknesses, pay particular attention to using tentative language.

4 Drawing to a Close

The final chapter of your dissertation draws together everything you have said earlier and completes the picture for your readers. At one level it should prove relatively easy to write as you will have finished all your research and will be totally familiar with your findings: by the time you come to write the conclusion you will be the expert in the particular area you chose to investigate. At another level, however, it may prove a challenge as you will need to link everything you have said earlier with the ideas you present in your conclusion, ensuring that you address all the issues and/or questions you raised in your introduction. This chapter begins by looking at what steps you need to take to produce a conclusion that is communicatively successful.

WRITING A CONCLUSION: MAIN STEPS

To a large extent, the content and organisation of your final chapter will be determined by the purpose of your study and what has come before in your dissertation. However, the overall purpose of any conclusion is the same: to show how the researcher has attempted to fill the gap in knowledge that was identified at the outset of the research and to clarify to what extent the study has been successful. If we return to the analogy of the building renovation that we introduced in Chapter 1, we can see how a dissertation's conclusion can be viewed in the same way as the end of a renovation process. We noted earlier that the introduction to your dissertation can be seen as an explanation of the changes you intend to make to improve a building that is in need of renovation. Before you explain the changes, you need first of all to describe your building at the outset of your project and point out its deficiencies. The main body of the dissertation consists of a detailed description of the renovations carried out. When the renovations are completed, you need to consult the list of problems that you initially noted to ensure that you have dealt with them all, in so far as you were able to. In the same way, in the conclusion to your dissertation you need to remind the readers of the initial state of the building by revisiting its deficiencies and then to summarise the information on the renovations you have carried out so that the readers can see the building in its finished state. To be entirely honest, you will also point out along the way any problems that you were not able to solve or mistakes that you made. But the story does not end there. Being an ambitious builder, you will also be planning an extension to your building, or even a new building that will be better than the finished one! And you will certainly want to tell your readers of your ideas for this future work.

We can see from the above that there are four aspects to consider when looking at the completed renovation:

1. look back at the original state of the building and explain the renovations carried out;
2. stress how many of the problems have been dealt with and how the building has improved;
3. acknowledge any problems still remaining or mistakes made;
4. plan for the future.

If we consider these four aspects from the point of view of the conclusion to your dissertation, we can look at them as four basic steps that need to be taken in your writing. (Compare these with the four steps you take in introducing your dissertation.) We call these steps the '4S' model; this is one of the most common models for a conclusion.

Table 4.1   Four basic steps to take in writing a conclusion (the '4S' model)

Step 1: Summarise your research
Step 2: Spell out your contribution
Step 3: State the limitations of your study
Step 4: Suggest potential areas of further research

The following conclusion from a journal article on real estate research shows how the writers conclude their paper by following through these four steps.

EXAMPLE 4.1

This study investigates whether houses located on rear-entry alleyways should sell for less than otherwise identical properties with traditional front-entry driveways. [1] The regression results suggest that the alleyway subdivision design discounts sale prices by 5% all else held equal. [2] Why? Because alleyways can attract criminal activities and greatly reduce the size of the homeowner's backyard. [3] As well, they are often poorly maintained, unsightly, cluttered with debris and inconvenient, so many residents park their vehicles on the street, thereby creating traffic congestion. [4]

While the findings of the research suggest that there are diseconomies associated with the rear-entry alleyway design, one element in the New Urbanism contemporary neighborhood design is, in fact, the alleyway that emphasizes compactness and a return to traditional neighborhood values. [5] New Urbanists believe that it helps overcome urban sprawl and encourages less reliance on automobiles, while critics counter that New Urbanism attempts to alter human behavior through design, it creates more traffic problems than it solves, its densities are too low to support public transportation and it does not offer consumers enough housing choices. [6] These findings hopefully will influence New Urbanism subdivision designers to reconsider alleyways in favor of traditional suburban parking. [7]

The results of this study may be, in part, a function of this sample, but the implications are clear for appraisers, developers, New

Urbanists and other real estate participants. [8] Subdivision design contributes to overall value. [9] Additional subdivision design research is recommended, both to confirm the findings of this investigation and to determine whether other elements of design (e.g., sidewalks, culverts vs. curb-and gutter drainage) affect value as well. [10]

Steps	Sentence(s)
1. Summary of the main findings of the research	1–6
2. Spelling out of the contribution	7, 8 (final part) and 9
3. Statement of limitations	8 (initial part)
4. Suggestions for further research	10

In Example 4.1 all four steps are apparent, but we should note that Step 3 (limitations) is not clearly separated from Step 2; it is almost as though the writer stepped up to Step 3 and then back down again. It is, in fact, important to note that there is considerable variation in the order in which these steps are taken. Many conclusions in journal articles do not follow the order suggested in Table 4.1, although in dissertations the order tends to be much more standard. Example 4.2 below, from a journal article in language teaching research, shows another conclusion which follows the '4S' model in terms of the number of steps, but the order is not that suggested in Table 4.1.

EXAMPLE 4.2

The present study is one in a series that has probed the nature of task-based performance. It has shown that the conditions under which tasks are completed can have a marked effect on the resultant nature of the performance. [1] The study has confirmed the generally beneficial effects of pre-task preparation, particularly planning. [2] Encouragingly, from the pedagogic point of view, there seems to be a clear role for the teacher in the way such pre-tasks are carried out – it does not have to be with learners always operating independently. [3] The results obtained suggest that teacher-based planning is as effective as solitary planning, but that both of these conditions are superior to group-based planning – at least, as that was implemented in the present study. [4]

But the present study has only explored the effects of immediate task-linked manipulations. [5] If the wider pedagogic goal is the sustained and balanced development of learners' interlanguage systems, it is important to be able to discuss how the effects of particular tasks might connect to longer term development. [6] In this respect, if balanced progress means higher levels of complexity, accuracy and fluency, it may be speculated that teachers need, as part of their armoury of pedagogic decision-making, information such as which conditions and which tasks may bring about such sustained balanced development. [7] It is to be hoped that the present research has made a contribution in that regard, although it is clear that, having established some of the influences on immediate performance, a priority in future research will be to explore what happens to interlanguage development during more extended pedagogic interventions. [8]

Steps	Sentence(s)
5. Summary of the main findings of the research	1–4
6. Spelling out of the contribution	7 and 8 (first part)
7. Statement of limitations	5–6
8. Suggestions for further research	8 (final part)

Other Models

The two examples we have seen above are illustrations of the '4S' model of conclusions, but '3S' and '2S' models are also frequently found. The '3S' model omits any reference to limitations. This is a possible variation in a dissertation which has already dealt with the limitations of the study at some length in the discussion chapter. The '2S' model is quite common in dissertations reporting on non-experimental research in which you analyse a text or philosophical stand. Such a dissertation might have only the first two steps from the '4S' model, where you summarise your research and highlight your contribution towards the end. You may not consider explicitly the limitations of your study or make suggestions for future research. An illustration of this is seen in Example 4.3 which is the Table of Contents for the final chapter of a philosophy PhD.

EXAMPLE 4.3

Chapter 8. Conclusion
    8.1 The Problem
    8.2 Overview of the Background Theory
    8.3 The Two Ideals

The first section of this chapter (8.1) reiterates the problem addressed in the study, while section 8.2 contextualises this problem in light of the theory that has been discussed earlier in the dissertation. These two sections form Step 1 (summary of the research) and the final section (8.3) forms Step 2 (spelling out of the contribution). The final section actually starts with a restatement of the research questions and then goes on as follows:

> On the basis of the interpretive theory presented in the preceding chapters, I can now suggest a series of answers to these questions.

The author then explains how his conclusions concerning the problem addressed contribute a new understanding to the field. By restating the research questions and explicitly signalling that answers to the questions are to follow, the author clearly links the introduction and conclusion of the dissertation together.

Note:
Some dissertations, particularly those in the humanities, do not devote an entire chapter to the conclusion. The conclusion may be the last section of the final chapter. This section, which may or may not be signalled by a subheading, still needs to draw the work to a close, summarising the findings and highlighting the contribution.

TASK 4.1

Read through the following conclusion from an article on the history of interior architecture and identify the four different steps.

This study set out to consider the extent to which developments in the medieval lifestyle affected the interiors of the time. [1] The findings indicated that both political developments and modifications in the mode of warfare brought about numerous changes in the lifestyle of the people and corresponding changes to the interiors of castles, which were the main residential establishments of the day. [2] Amongst the most important changes were the relocation of the fireplace from the centre of the room to a side wall, the introduction of heavier more permanent furniture, the establishment of specific rooms in the home for different activities and larger windows. [3]
One of the most significant results from this study is the identification of the growth and subsequent collapse of the feudal system as the source of many of the internal changes in castles. [4] The communal living encouraged by the interdependence of different social classes during the feudal period began to disappear as feudalism gave way to nationalism. [5] By the twelfth century, the power of the nobles was beginning to give way to that of the kings as a sense of nationhood grew in Europe. [6] The lords, who had earlier spent considerable time and resources on expanding their territories and establishing their command, had moved into a period when consolidating their position as masters of their existing territory was essential. [7] They began, therefore, to add more storeys to their existing castles rather than to acquire new land and build new castles. [8] The height of a castle came to be seen as a symbol of power, dominating the countryside around. [9] These additional storeys led to a greater physical separation of the lord's family from the workers and the whole style of living began to change. [10]
Another significant finding relates to the change created in the interiors of castles by the introduction of the use of gunpowder as a means of warfare. [11] The use of gunpowder revolutionised the

whole style of warfare and left castles much less impregnable to attack. [12] With this change, the castle, in fact, lost its role as a defensive unit. [13] Thus, the requirement for small slit windows was obviated and daylight could finally enter the lives of the castle's inhabitants. [14] Glass then became much more commonplace in windows to keep out the draughts and window seats became popular as they afforded those within, particularly the women of the castles, ample opportunities to watch the world go by. [15] The castle had finally ceased to function as primarily a fortified residence, but was more properly a home where the lord's families lived a settled and relatively comfortable life. [16]

This study has focused only on the changes that developments in lifestyle brought to the castles of medieval times. [17] Studies need now to be extended to consider how the interiors of public buildings and churches were affected. [18] It would be interesting to discover whether or not the increasing amount of daylight that could enter people's homes and social life was also evident in administrative and religious life; perhaps the increasing daylight was a suitable physical enlightenment to symbolise the coming of the Renaissance that was soon to light up the spirit of Europe. [19]

WRITING A CONCLUSION: ADDITIONAL STEPS

Considering the Implications of Your Study

As indicated in the opening of this chapter, the content of your conclusion will largely be determined by the overall purpose of your research. Your research may have important implications which you will want to articulate. If these implications are extensive, you may have a separate chapter between the Discussion and Conclusion chapters. However, if the implications are too few to warrant a chapter on their own, you will normally address the implications of your study in the conclusion, immediately after highlighting your contribution, although some authors prefer to deal with the limitations first, before addressing the implications. In Example 4.4 taken from a clinical physiology journal article on exercise, we can see how the clinical implications of the study are presented.

EXAMPLE 4.4

Clinical Implications

The results from the present study show that in sedentary, overweight adults, a 9-month exercise training program with a relatively large weekly exercise dose resulted in a significant and prolonged improvement in fasting plasma glucose. [1] The decrease in FPG was maintained after 1 month of detraining. [2] Whether this was related to the prolonged improvement in insulin sensitivity, which was still 24% above pretraining level at this time point, or to some insulin-independent mechanism(s), is not clear. [3] These data provide evidence that both acute and chronic improvements in carbohydrate metabolism result from long-term exercise training. [4] Concurrent with these changes were significant improvements in blood lipids and aerobic capacity. [5] These findings have clinical significance for the role of regular exercise in preventing the development of insulin resistance and glucose intolerance in individuals at risk for diabetes and cardiovascular diseases. [6]

The above paragraph, the final one of the journal article, can be analysed as follows:

Steps	Sentences
1. Summary of findings	1–3
2. Spelling out of the contribution	4–5
3. Statement of clinical implications	6

We should notice that this is a '3S' conclusion, where no limitations are considered, as they have been discussed in the previous section of the paper, and suggestions for future research are replaced by a statement of clinical implications.

Making Recommendations

Another common feature found towards the end of a report on research is a set of recommendations. As with implications, if you have extensive recommendations, these may form a separate chapter between the Discussion and Conclusion chapters, but otherwise, like implications, recommendations usually come after the contribution, but may be dealt with after the limitations. In Example 4.5, which is the final section of a research article on 'protecting wetlands' from a journal in environmental management, we have an illustration of a conclusion which ends with the recommendations.

Example 4.5

Recommendations

One major policy recommendation arising from the quantitative evaluation approach in this paper is to realise that the protection of wetlands is not merely an ecological issue but involves a number of crucially important aspects of social and political decision-making processes. [1] If the protection of ecologically valuable wetlands is accepted as an important public objective, the influence and interests of stakeholders in the primary sector and tourist and recreational industries have to be taken into account. [2] So far there has been no consistent and transparent decision framework that is able to guarantee a transparent and well-balanced political process. [3]

Recent experiences regarding the Natura 2000 initiative set up by the European Union indicate that the federal system in Austria leads to very different processes and policy decisions. [4] Based on such findings and on the quantitative results of the current paper, there seems to be a need for new public valuation tools and decision-making processes which include stakeholders' participation and consultation with the aim of exploring opportunities for more ecologically oriented wetlands protection policy. [5]

A transparent and participatory framework has a number of advantages for decision-makers. [6] First, involving stakeholders can be considered as a tool to collect (local and regional) tacit knowledge.

[7] Second, the decision-making process itself might be perceived as being more 'fair' and democratic, which can reduce the cost of policy implementation. [8] Third, within a transparent public decision-making process, the individual interests of pressure groups (such as the economic interests of certain sectors) might turn out to be of less importance when compared with other (ecological and economic) interests. [9] Thus, policy-makers can be made more responsible for their decisions and are not able to hide behind opaque decision-making processes [10].

Steps	Sentence(s)
1. Recommendation	1
2. Consequence of recommendation	2
3. Statement of need for future research	3–5
4. Advantages of proposed new system	7–9
5. Advantage of adopting recommendation	10

A Positive Ending

The sample conclusions that we have examined so far have all been from journal articles and are, therefore, of necessity, brief. The conclusion to a dissertation, however, being generally a whole chapter, albeit usually the shortest one, will be several pages long. This being the case, it is common for writers to have what seems at first sight to be an extra step in the conclusion: concluding remarks. We can see an illustration of this in Example 4.6 below which shows the Table of Contents from the closing chapter of a dissertation in applied linguistics.

EXAMPLE 4.6

CHAPTER 6. CONCLUSION
6.1 Summary
6.2 Major significant results
6.3 A new model. Effects of task type and source of control on negotiation of meaning

In this Table of Contents the standard '4S' order has been followed, but Step 2 (contribution) has been divided into two parts, 6.2 and 6.3, and one of the additional steps (implications for teaching) has been combined with Step 4 (further research).

Subsection 6 *(Concluding remarks)*, which appears to be an extra step, is actually a restatement of Step 2 – *Contribution*. In this section, the author wishes to emphasise the contribution the research has made to knowledge in the field and, therefore, restates the contribution in order to end on a positive note. You should always remember, as we indicated in Chapter 1, to constantly think about your readers' needs. At this point in reading your dissertation, what your readers need is to be convinced that it was all worthwhile and that you have not only dealt with the issues you raised at the beginning of your study but that you have made a real contribution to the field. If you end on a positive note, your readers will close your dissertation with a sense of satisfaction.

TASK 4.2

Read through the following concluding sections of journal articles and analyse them in terms of the steps the authors take in drawing the paper to a close. Text 1 is from an article in a medical journal, Text 2 from a literature journal and Text 3 from a sociology journal.

Text 1

(The end of the final section of the paper, entitled *Discussion*.)

Since there were only 19 females among our patient group, this may reflect the possible unsuitability of urine as a source of gonococcal antigens in females. [1] However, conclusions should only be drawn by further sampling from a larger female population. [2] Furthermore, the urine specimens collected for this study were only random samples. [3] The use of first-voided morning urine as an alternative sample for diagnosis may improve the sensitivity. [4] The traditional sampling procedure for diagnosing gonorrhoea requires swabbing of the endo-urethra for infected urethral epithelial cells. [5] This procedure is unpleasant and invasive, especially for male patients; it is also inconvenient for epidemiological studies of asymptomatic infections. [6] The use of urine, although less sensitive than urethral swabs for diagnosis of gonorrhoea, has advantages because the collection of the former is much more convenient and non-invasive. [7] With these initial encouraging results, urine should be further investigated as an alternative specimen to genital swabs for diagnosis of gonorrhoea in asymptomatic male patients. [8] In summary, GonozymeTM appears to be an acceptable test for detection of gonococcal antigens in genital swab specimens from males and females. [9] The speed and high sensitivity of GonozymeTM enables this test to be used as a potential alternative method to culture for diagnosis of gonorrhoea – especially for under-developed countries or small laboratories, where specimens often have to be sent to distant laboratories for culture. [10] Urine has the potential to be used instead of urethral swabs for diagnosis of gonorrhoea in males, but further evaluation and improvement are necessary before it can be recommended for use in routine screening. [11]

Text 2

To conclude, I feel that the standard master narrative of modern literary history is so limited and so flawed that it should be extensively augmented or abandoned altogether as an explanatory construct. [1] Twentieth century narrative is too diverse, multiform and overdetermined to be reduced to a simple formula within a chronological sequence. [2] The realism/modernism/postmodernism progression simply does not correctly describe literary practice in this century. [3] A more accurate, rhizomatic model shows instead five distinct significant narrative poetics – realism, postmodernism, high modernism, expressionism, and romance – that continuously fluctuate, battle against, merge with, and interanimate each other dialogically every decade. [4]

The urge toward teleology, one that cannot be resisted by literary polemicists and authors of manifestoes, must be regularly contested by literary historians. [5] No one believes anymore that science steadily progresses towards an unchanging goal, or that historical events can adequately be contained within the form of a single linear narrative. [6] Why then should we ever assume that comparable narrative structures are able to embrace modern literature or critical theory? [7] The rich mass of narrative fiction of this century demands a more capacious, flexible and open-minded account. [8] I hope the model I have presented here suggests a more useful and accurate – if also necessarily provisional – way of conceptualizing it in all its messy heterogeneity. [9]

Text 3

(The final paragraph, of the paper, entitled *Conclusions and Recommendations*.)

Retractions should be considered seriously and impartially as new evidence. [1] They are worth investigating fully, in some cases with a full videotaped Memorandum of Good Practice interview. [2] The impact of child protection investigations and interventions on a child and family should be reckoned and their agenda appreciated when planning such. [3] It should be particularly appreciated that perceived powerful protectors may engender a further sense of powerlessness in a child. [4] This may prompt the child to try to put the clock back to the status quo before allegations were made. [5] A careful 'statement validity analysis' of both allegations and full story of the retraction process may offer strong clues as to the validity of the fabrication of one and not the other. [6]

WRITING A CONCLUSION: LANGUAGE FEATURES

Subordination

One important grammatical choice that you will need to make as you are writing your dissertation concerns what information you want to include in a subordinate as opposed to a main clause. A main clause is one that can be understood on its own without any additional information. A subordinate clause cannot be understood on its own; it needs another clause, i.e. a main clause, to complete its meaning. One particular type of subordinate clause, a clause of concession, is of particular importance in academic writing and perhaps nowhere more so than in the conclusion. A clause of concession is one that concedes, that is, acknowledges, the existence of a fact or point of view that is in opposition to the fact or view expressed in the main clause. Example 4.7 shows a clause of concession italicised:

EXAMPLE 4.7

> *Although the house has beautiful views and is in a dream location,* it is far too expensive for its size and there is no garden.

The main points that the writer wishes to make about the house in Example 4.7 are negative: the expense and the lack of a garden. To be quite fair, he concedes that the house has positive features, but he wishes to dismiss these in his argument, so they are placed in a subordinate clause.

It is also possible to use a phrase, rather than a clause, of concession in the same way. We can see the preposition *despite* used in Example 4.8 to introduce a phrase describing a man's negative aspects, whilst the main clause concentrates our attention on the positive side of his character.

EXAMPLE 4.8

Despite the fact that he has a criminal past and little experience in this line of work, he seems to have reformed and he learns quickly.

Where you choose to place a piece of information will generally depend upon the relative importance you wish to give to that information. It is important to realise that placing information in a subordinate rather than a main clause may completely change the meaning of a sentence and this is particularly true with clauses of concession. We can see below an example of a situation in a murder trial, in a court of law, where the placing of information in a subordinate clause could be a matter of life and death.

EXAMPLE 4.9

(a) *Although there is no evidence to connect him to the crime,* he had a strong motive.

(b) *Although he had a strong motive,* there is no evidence to connect him to the crime.

In (a) the fact that there is no evidence against the accused is being acknowledged, but dismissed (in the subordinate clause) because he had a motive, as noted in the main clause. In (b) the lack of evidence is being highlighted by being placed in the main clause. A prosecutor would use sentence (a) to try and convince the jury that the accused is guilty, while (b) would be used by the defence to introduce reasonable doubt.

The following example (Example 4.10) from an academic context demonstrates the importance of carefully choosing which information to place in the concession phrase.

EXAMPLE 4.10

(a) In conclusion, *despite the limitations described in the paragraph above,* this study contributes to a growing literature on individual creativity in organizations and provides support for an interactionist approach.

(b) In conclusion, *despite the fact that this study contributes to a growing literature on individual creativity in organizations and provides support for an interactionist approach,* it has numerous limitations.

In (a) the author is acknowledging the fact that there are limitations to the study, but highlighting the contribution of this study to the field in the main clause. In (b) the writer is downplaying the importance of that contribution and drawing the readers' attention to the limitations of the study. Sentence (b) would clearly not be a positive or satisfactory ending to a dissertation.

TASK 4.3

Compare the following pairs of sentences and consider how the meaning of the sentence changes when the message in the subordinate clause is changed.

Text 1

(a) Although there is no doubt that the ISO standard provides a more definite and practical way to establish a quality management system, the use of ISO 9000 is highly controversial.

(b) Although the use of ISO 9000 is highly controversial, there is no doubt that the ISO standard provides a more definite and practical way to establish a quality management system.

Text 2

(a) The use of urine, although less sensitive than urethral swabs for diagnosis of gonorrhoea, has advantages because the collection of the former is much more convenient and non-invasive.

(b) Although the use of urine has advantages as its collection is much more convenient and non-invasive, it is less sensitive than urethral swabs for diagnosis of gonorrhoea.

Before You Finish

So now you have come to the end of your dissertation. The last chapter is written and you are ready to submit. Well, not quite! Before you reach that truly final stage, you need to summarise all that you have said and done in the abstract. This chapter now moves on to look at this final step in the writing process.

WRITING THE ABSTRACT

The abstract is the last section of a dissertation to be written. It is written after the research has been completed and the writer knows exactly what is contained in the body of the text. It is a summary of the text and it informs readers of what can be found in the dissertation and in what order, functioning rather as an overall signpost for the reader. Although it is the last part of a dissertation to be written, it is generally one of the first a reader will look at. Indeed, if the abstract is not well written, it may be the only part of the dissertation a reader will look at!

Content and Organisation of an Abstract

When readers look at an abstract, they want to find answers to the following questions:
1. What was the purpose of the research?
2. Why was the research carried out?
3. How was the research conducted?
4. What did the researcher discover?

An abstract should ideally present information that will answer these questions, following the order in which the information is presented in the dissertation. We now examine Example 4.11 below, taken from an article in a journal of real estate research, to see if these questions are answered.

EXAMPLE 4.11

At the centre of the debate on racially induced price differentials in housing is the issue of discrimination. [1] This research studies the impact that ethnic as well as racial composition in a neighbourhood exerts on value. [2] In an attempt to extend previous efforts, aggregate data is used to study the effects of discrimination and lending bias on residential real estate in Houston, Texas. [3] The data do not support allegations of systematic bias in the mortgage lending process. [4]

[81 words]

Question	Answer
1. **What was the purpose of the research?**	*To investigate how ethnic and racial factors effect lending for mortgages.* [Sentences 2 and 3]
2. **Why was the research carried out?**	*Because the question of racial discrimination in housing prices has been raised.* [Sentence 1]
3. **How was the research conducted?**	*Aggregate data on residential real estate in Houston, Texas, was collected.* [Sentence 3]
4. **What did the researcher discover?**	*There is no systematic bias in mortgage lending based on racial factors.* [Sentence 4]

We should note that in this abstract there is no specific statement to say **why** the research was conducted. It is, however, stated in Sentence 1 that there is a current debate on the issue of racial discrimination in housing. As any type of discrimination is usually a sign of a problem situation, we can say that the justification for this study is implicit, in that the study was initiated by the wish to solve a problem or settle a debate: the existence of a problem, or lack of knowledge in an area, being a common justification for any research. An explicit statement of justification may be omitted in an abstract, both in a dissertation and a journal article, if the reason for the research is obvious from the purpose.

We can also note from the analysis of this abstract that detailed findings are not presented because the findings are implied from the conclusion that is drawn. In the abstract to a journal article a writer is usually extremely limited in the number of words allowed; it is common for the limit for a journal article to be set at around 150 words. Where limitations force some information to be omitted, the specific findings are often not noted because, as with the justification, they can be implied. In a dissertation abstract, however, the findings are never omitted as they are an essential element of the summary; in fact, they regularly comprise a large proportion of the abstract. We can see that this is the case in Example 4.12, which is the abstract from a PhD dissertation in social work.

EXAMPLE 4.12

Self-determination of young adults with mild mental handicap: Implications for education and vocational preparation

This study sets out to examine, from an insider perspective, people with mild mental handicap concerning their pre-vocational and vocational experience. [1] A qualitative methodological approach was taken and a semi-structured interviewing technique for triangulation of data sources was adopted. [2] Both cross-sectional and longitudinal data were collected from an opportunity sample of 66 individuals with mild mental handicap aged between 15 to 29 years and a representative sample of non-handicapped counterparts (n=37). [3] Professionals from special schools and employment placement programmes, and family members of participants with mild mental handicap were also interviewed. [4] Documents related to vocational preparation for participants with mild mental handicap were examined. [5] A constant comparative method and content analysis were used to analyse data collected. [6]

Findings of this study indicated that the participants with mild mental handicap and their non-handicapped counterparts were capable of articulating job preferences. [7] Both groups of participants sought employment for similar reasons and both encountered some difficulties in obtaining their preferred jobs as they had limited available work options. [8] This seems to suggest that conceptual models concerning vocational development of people without disabilities could be applied, with minor modifications, also to people with mild mental handicap. [9] The major contrast between their pre-vocational and vocational experience was in the area of self-determination. [10] About three-quarters of the participants with mild mental handicap were not perceived by their families, schools and employment placement programmes as capable of making decisions regarding post-school placement and employment. [11] This study, however, provided strong evidence that approximately one-quarter of the participants with mild mental handicap displayed self-determining behaviour. [12]

Arising from these data, a triad empowerment model is proposed to enable people with mental handicap, their families and professionals within the whole school system and vocational services to develop a partnership where such people are encouraged to take up self-determining roles. [13] Within the context of partnership, a two-level approach for vocational preparation is suggested to facilitate the school-to-work transition for people with mental handicap. [14] This study supports the self-determination of such people to be part of decision making concerning the quality of education and vocational services being planned for them. [15]

If we analyse this abstract to see which sentences answer the questions that an abstract should answer, we have the following breakdown:

Question	Where answered
1. What was the purpose of the research?	Sentence 1
2. Why was the research carried out?	?
3. How was the research conducted?	Sentences 2–6
4. What did the researcher discover?	Sentences 7, 8, 10, 11 and 12

We can notice here that, as in Example 4.11, there is no specific statement of **why** this research was carried out. We can, however, imply from the purpose that there is a lack of knowledge about how the subjects of this study [*people with mild mental handicap*] view the topic that is being studied [*pre-vocational and vocational experiences*] and, therefore, this research needs to be carried out.

We can also notice that there are several sentences that are not included in the analysis as answers to the questions given, i.e. Sentences 9 and 13–15. Sentence 9 tells the readers what conclusions can be drawn from the findings; Sentences 13 and 14 put forward recommendations the researcher is making and the last sentence, 15, highlights the contribution of the research. It is usual to include these elements in a dissertation abstract, if indeed the dissertation has recommendations to make, although they are often omitted from the abstract to a research journal article, due to word limits.

TASK 4.4

Look at the abstract below, which is taken from an article in a criminology journal, and answer Questions 1–5 on p. 117.

Recidivism reduction is an important objective of many correctional programs. [1] Recent survey data suggest that boot camp prisons (also known as shock incarceration programs) are no exception. [2] In this study, we examine recidivism among boot camp completers in eight stages of community supervision. [3] We then assess these recidivism patterns in light of how one or more comparison groups in each state perform. [4] For most states, two or more recidivism measures (such as arrest and revocation) are employed. [5] The analysis suggests that those who complete boot camps do not inevitably perform either better or worse than their comparison group counterparts. [6] Rather, program effectiveness has to be judged on a state-by-state basis. [7]
[110 words]

Questions:
1. What was the purpose of the research?
2. Why was the research carried out?
3. How was the research conducted?
4. What did the researcher discover?
5. Is there any additional information given, other than the answers to the questions?

LENGTH OF AN ABSTRACT

The length of a dissertation abstract is usually prescribed by your institution. The minimum number of words is generally around 200 and the maximum 500. As you may be summarising as many as 80,000 words and you must include all the essential points, it is necessary to express yourself both clearly and concisely, with no redundant words or expressions.

TASK 4.5

Examine the two versions below of an abstract from an article on interior design and note what has been changed/removed from Version B to shorten the abstract from 129 to 99 words, assuming the maximum length prescribed for this abstract to be 100 words. Why do you think the words/phrases removed from Version A were redundant?

Version A

Robert Adam *has long been* acknowledged as one of the leading style innovators of the Neo-Classical period in interior design *in Europe*. Little attention has been paid, however, to the *role* of his *friend and* drawing teacher, *Charles Louis* Clerisseau, *who was* a master of perspective drawings, *in influencing* Adam's designs. This study examines the extant records of Clerisseau's work, along with *lengthy* correspondence between the two men *relating to several of Adam's architectural interiors*. The findings suggest that, while Clerisseau was not, *in fact*, the originator of *any of* Adam's design concepts, he made numerous suggestions on Adam's *first* drafts, based on which Adam modified his schemes. *In light of these findings, it seems that* Clerisseau should perhaps be given greater recognition for his contributions to Adam's interiors. [129 words]

Version B

Robert Adam is acknowledged as one of the leading style innovators of the Neo-Classical period in interior design. Little attention has been paid, however, to the influence of his drawing teacher, Clerisseau, a master of perspective drawings, on Adam's designs. This study examines the extant records of Clerisseau's work, along with correspondence between the two men. The findings suggest that, while Clerisseau was not the originator of Adam's design concepts, he made numerous suggestions on Adam's drafts, based on which Adam modified his schemes. Clerisseau should perhaps be given greater recognition for his contributions to Adam's interiors. [99 words]

TASK 4.6

The abstract below, which is taken from an article on real estate research, would be considered too long for many journals; it has 285 words. Try to rewrite it using a maximum of 200 words.

Abstract. The Home Mortgage Disclosure Act (HMDA) mandates the reporting of mortgage loan applications. [1] Nearly all studies of mortgage lending patterns done in recent years rely on the data collected under HMDA. [2] However, not all mortgages are reported under HMDA. [3] Understanding the relationship between HMDA coverage and neighborhood characteristics is particularly important because neighborhood rates of applications and loan originations from HMDA are used by many analysts to measure neighborhood lending activity. [4] If HMDA coverage rates vary systematically with neighborhood characteristics, then studies that use these neighborhood characteristics to explain lending activity will yield biased results. [5]

This paper presents the results of an analysis that attempts to estimate the fraction of mortgage activity that is reported under HMDA, and examines how HMDA coverage rates vary with the racial and income characteristics of the neighborhood. [6] The basic idea for this analysis is simple; identify a group of loans from an independent (non-HMDA) source and count the fraction of those loans that appear in the HMDA data. [7] Our independent source for loans is the loans purchased by Freddie Mac during 1992 and 1993; counts of these loans are compared with counts of loans reported as sold to Freddie Mac in the 1992 and 1993 HMDA datasets. [8] The major finding of the analysis is that the HMDA dataset for 1992 is estimated to contain only around 70% of the total mortgage loans, and the coverage rate only improves to 75% in 1993, despite the increased reporting requirements for 1993. [9] Both the 1992 and 1993 HMDA files exhibit substantial variability in coverage across census tracts and lenders, but the direction of bias is consistent. [10] Measured HMDA coverage rates are higher in lower income census tracts, relative to higher income census tracts. [11]

WRITING AN ABSTRACT: LANGUAGE FEATURES

Tense

There are two ways of viewing what you are doing when you write an abstract. You can see the writing as a description of the dissertation itself, i.e. the document that the abstract is summarising, or you can see the writing as a summary of the research that is reported in that document. If you take the first approach, you will tend to use the **present simple** throughout the abstract, but if you favour the latter approach, you are likely to mix the **present simple** and the **past simple,** using each at different points in the abstract.

Let us start by considering the first approach, which sees the abstract as a description of an object. When you are describing an object or a scene that you are looking at, the usual tense to use is the **present simple** because what you are really doing is listing facts about the object or the scene. We can see this in the example below:

EXAMPLE 4.13

> The building in the background *is* the highest in Asia. It *has* 88 storeys, the top 10 of which *belong* to the Hyatt Hotel chain. There *is* a revolving restaurant at the top and the views over the city from there *are* stunning. Diners *can see* the entire city centre on a clear day.

The same is true when you tell someone the story in a book or a film; what you are doing is describing what exists in the book, rather than events that took place at some point in time. This is illustrated in the next example.

EXAMPLE 4.14

> The story *starts* at the end of the war when a man called Graham *returns* to his hometown and *finds* that his house has been destroyed. When he *goes* to see the authorities he *discovers* that his family is listed as missing, so he sets out to find them. Most of the rest of the action *takes place* in the countryside where he *travels* from village to village in search of his parents and sisters.

If you see an abstract in this way, you are not telling the readers what actions you set out to perform and what you did; you are describing what exists in the article/dissertation that follows the abstract, and you will use the **present simple** in the same way as above. We can see that is the case in the two abstracts we studied earlier, Example 4.11 and Task 4.4.

Text from Example 4.11

At the centre of the debate on racially induced price differentials in housing *is* the issue of discrimination. [1] This research *studies* the impact that ethnic as well as racial composition in a neighbourhood *exerts* on value. [2] In an attempt to extend previous efforts aggregate data *is used* to study the effects of discrimination and lending bias on residential real estate in Houston, Texas. [3] The data *do not support* allegations of systematic bias in the mortgage lending process. [4]

Text from Task 4.4

Recidivism reduction *is* an important objective of many correctional programs. [1] Recent survey data *suggest* that boot camp prisons (also known as shock incarceration programs) *are* no exception. [2] In this study, we *examine* recidivism among boot camp completers in eight stages of community supervision. [3] We then *assess* these recidivism patterns in light of how one or more comparison groups in each state *perform*. [4] For most states, two or more recidivism measures (such as arrest and revocation) *are employed*. [5] The analysis *suggests* that those who complete boot camps *do not* inevitably *perform* either better or worse than their comparison group counterparts. [6] Rather, program effectiveness *has* to be judged on a state-by-state basis. [7]

If, however, you adopt the approach that an abstract is a summary of the research that is reported in that document, you will use different tenses for different parts of the abstract. In the dissertation abstract in Example 4.12, both **present simple** and **past simple** are used. The present is used for stating the purpose in the first sentence [*This study **sets out to**]* and for presenting the conclusions and recommendations in Sentences 9 and 13–15. The past is used to describe the method used and to present the individual findings. Below we can see another example of the mixed use of tenses in the abstract to an article in a journal of applied ergonomics.

EXAMPLE 4.15

Concerns *have arisen* that the keyboard *is* a causal factor in the development of work-related musculoskeletal disorders (WRMDS) among video display terminal operators (VDT). [1] A number of alternative keyboard designs *have been developed* with altered geometry in an effort to improve comfort in keyboard operation. [2] However, few data *are* available to substantiate whether these new keyboard designs *are* actually effective in reducing discomfort and musculoskeletal problems in users. [3] The purpose of this study *was* to provide data on the efficacy of certain alternative keyboard design features (e.g. splitting the keyboard in half, and laterally inclining the keyboard halves) in reducing fatigue and musculoskeletal discomfort among keyboard operators. [4] The study also *explored* the effects of these design features on performance. [5] Fifty subjects *performed* a text-entry task for one day on a standard keyboard, then *were assigned* to one of five keyboard conditions for an evaluation period of two days (i.e. 10 subjects/condition). [6] Outcome measures *included* performance (i.e. keystrokes/h, errors/h) and self-report measures of discomfort and fatigue. [7] The results *indicated* an initial decline in productivity when subjects *began* typing on two of the alternative keyboards, but these productivity losses *were recovered* within the two-day evaluation period. [8] The results also *indicated* no significant differences between keyboard conditions in discomfort and fatigue. [9] These results *suggest* a minimal impact of the keyboard design features examined in this study on productivity, comfort and fatigue, at least after two days of exposure. [10]

This abstract uses the **past simple** in Sentences 4–9, where the purpose, method and results are reported, and the **present simple** in Sentence 3, where the present lack of data is noted, and in Sentence 10 for the conclusion that is drawn. The **present perfect** is also used in the abstract, in Sentences 1 and 2, which establish what the situation is at the outset of the research, i.e. they bring the readers up to date with the current state of affairs which led to the research. (This use of the present perfect was noted in Chapter 1 when discussing how the research gap is established.)

Decisions on which tense to use in an abstract may be left up to the individual writer, but often the choice is prescribed by the discipline. You should look carefully at abstracts in your discipline to see which tense is used in dissertations and you should examine journals before you submit an article, to find out if there is a house style with regard to tense use in abstracts.

TASK 4.7

Find two journal abstracts in your field and analyse them in terms of the verb tense they use.

Bringing It All Together

Points to remember:

❖ There must be an explicit link between the introduction and the conclusion of your dissertation. In the conclusion you will need to ensure that you have addressed the main issues and questions you identified at the beginning of your dissertation. You will need to show that you have filled the research gap you identified (at least in part).

❖ You should highlight your contribution and show how your research is innovative — how it has added to existing knowledge.

❖ You should end your dissertation on a positive note. In the final paragraph you should avoid tentative language.

❖ The abstract *must* tell readers what was done in the research undertaken and what was discovered.

❖ The abstract *may* also tell readers why and how the research was done.

❖ The present simple and the past simple are the commonest tenses to use when writing your abstract. Use whichever your discipline favours.

❖ It is necessary to be concise in your abstract as the number of words allowed is very limited.

Concluding Academic Papers and Writing Abstracts

There is considerable variability in what one includes in the conclusion and abstract to an academic paper and this is often dictated by the journal itself. It is therefore a good idea to browse through the journal you wish to submit a paper to, in order to see how other authors have concluded their work and how their abstracts are written. It is also a good idea to read the instructions to authors carefully to see if there are any specifications relating to these parts of the paper.

Most scientific journals follow the IMRAD formula (Introduction, Materials and Method, Results and Discussion) and so the conclusion is the last part of the Discussion section. In the social sciences it is usually expected that there will be a separate section that concludes the paper. However, this section is not always entitled 'Conclusion'. A statement of implications or of future research needs may form the last part of a paper, but recommendations, which are more often addressed to professional bodies than academic audiences, are not so often included. Since journal articles are by necessity considerably shorter and more narrowly focussed than a dissertation, authors need to be more selective as to what they include in their conclusion. There must, however, be a direct link between the introduction and the conclusion in the same way as there is this link in a dissertation.

Follow-up Tasks

1. Go back to a term paper you have written and write an appropriate abstract for it. Try to make your abstract no more than 1/20th of the length of your paper, i.e. for a 2500-word paper your abstract should be around 120 words.

2. Look at the concluding section in two or three dissertations and analyse them in terms of the models suggested in this chapter. Are you clear from the conclusions what the writers did in their research, what they found and what contributions to knowledge they made?

5 Structuring and Signposting

Having considered the individual parts of the dissertation in earlier chapters, we can now look at putting the parts together. We indicated in Chapter 1 that there are different ways of doing this as there are different types of dissertation structure. In this chapter we first look at the different types of dissertation that are commonly found and then we discuss signposting, which is an important means of helping readers through your text.

STRUCTURING THE DISSERTATION

The structure of your dissertation will depend on the purpose and type of study you conduct, but it is likely to fall into one of the four basic types of dissertation described below. Factors which will affect the overall organisation and structure include:

- whether you are reporting on a single study or multiple studies;
- whether your research is experimental or topic-based;
- whether your dissertation is based on papers you have already published.

Table 5.1, illustrating **Type 1 and Type 2** dissertations, shows ways in which dissertations based on a single study are usually structured. The same basic structures may be used for reporting on multiple studies as illustrated in Table 5.2.

Table 5.1   Single study dissertations

Type 1:	Single study	Type 2:	Single study
Chapter 1	Introduction	**Chapter 1**	Introduction
Chapter 2	Materials and method(s)	**Chapter 2**	Literature Review
Chapter 3	Results	**Chapter 3**	Materials and method(s)
Chapter 4	Discussion	**Chapter 4**	Results
Chapter 5	Conclusion(s)	**Chapter 5**	Discussion
		Chapter 6	Conclusion(s)

Notice the brackets joining Chapters 4 and 5 of the Type 1 dissertation, indicating that these chapters are sometimes combined into a single chapter.

Table 5.2   Multiple study dissertations

Type 1:	Multiple studies	Type 2:	Multiple studies
Chapter 1	Introduction	**Chapter 1**	Introduction
Chapter 2	Study 1	**Chapter 2**	Background to study and Literature Review
	Introduction		
	Method(s)		
	Results		
	Discussion and conclusion(s)		
Chapter 3	Study 2	**Chapter 3**	Study 1
	Introduction		Introduction
	Method(s)		Method(s)
	Results		Results
	Discussion and conclusion(s)		Discussion and conclusion(s)
Chapter 4	Study 3	**Chapter 4**	Study 2
	Introduction		Introduction
	Method(s)		Method(s)
	Results		Results
	Discussion and conclusion(s)		Discussion and conclusion(s)
Chapter 5	Discussion	**Chapter 5**	Study 3
			Introduction
			Method(s)
			Results
			Discussion and conclusion(s)
Chapter 6	Conclusion(s)	**Chapter 6**	Discussion
		Chapter 7	Conclusion(s)

Although there is no prescribed number of studies for a dissertation to be considered complete, most frequently the number varies between two and four. In such multiple study dissertations, it is necessary to draw links between the different studies and that is the function of the introduction and of the discussion chapter (refer to Table 5.3), which you may combine with your conclusion as in a Type 1 single study dissertation.

Type 1 and Type 2 structures are common for experimental studies in the sciences and social sciences. In other types of research, especially in the humanities, **Type 3** structure, based around topics, is frequent. Table 5.3 illustrates such an organisational framework and provides an example from a PhD dissertation in philosophy. Each chapter here considers separate, though related, topics, but the threads from each are drawn together in a final concluding chapter.

Table 5.3 Topic-based organisation

Type 3:	Topic-based	Example (Philosophy)	
Chapter 1	Introduction	Chapter 1	Introduction
Chapter 2	Topic 1 Introduction Analysis/discussion of topic/text etc.	Chapter 2	Language, Thought and Action in Western Philosophy
Chapter 3	Topic 2 Introduction Analysis/discussion of topic/text etc.	Chapter 3	Names, Reality and Action
Chapter 4	Topic 3 Introduction Analysis/discussion of topic/text etc.	Chapter 4	Mohist Semantic Theory
" " " "		Chapter 5	Knowledge and Cognition
" " " "		Chapter 6	Persuasion
" " " "		Chapter 7	Theory of Action
Chapter X	Conclusion(s)	Chapter 8	Conclusion

The final type of dissertation (**Type 4**) based on published research articles is becoming increasingly common in some countries. Each article/chapter needs to stand on its own and will therefore have its own introduction, literature review, methods, results, discussion and conclusion. However, as noted in Chapter 1, the collected papers need an introductory chapter identifying the initial gap in research that links them together. Moreover, the findings need to be consolidated in an overall discussion, and a concluding chapter drawn from all the papers.

Table 5.4 Compilation of research articles

Chapter 1	Introduction	
Chapter 2	Background to the study	
Chapter 3	Research article 1	Introduction
		Literature Review
		Materials and Method(s)
		Results
		Discussion
		Conclusion(s)
Chapter 4	Research article 2	Introduction
		Literature Review
		Materials and Method(s)
		Results
		Discussion
		Conclusion(s)
Chapter 5	Research article 3	Introduction
		Literature Review
		Materials and Method(s)
		Results
		Discussion
		Conclusion(s)
Chapter 6	Discussion	
Chapter 7	Conclusion(s)	

TASK 5.1

Reflect on your own research. Which type of structure will you use for writing your dissertation? How does your organisation compare with that of your colleagues in your department? Do you have colleagues who are likely to use a different type of structure? Can you explain why a different structure would be more suitable for them?

SIGNPOSTING

Just as travellers expect to be guided along their route by road signs and will find the journey difficult and exasperating if the signposts are missing or misleading, readers expect to be guided along their way by signposts in the text and will find the reading task difficult and exasperating if the signposts are missing or misleading. The last thing both travellers and readers want is to lose their way and arrive at their destination in a bad temper.

It is the writer's responsibility to facilitate the reader's journey through a text by the use of signposts, or signals. The signals may be indicators of intention, describing what will be covered and in what order, or may be aids to memory, summarising what has been covered. Signposts could, then, be described as organisational markers which are used at different levels within a dissertation. To help you to use such signposts we now turn to look at both explicit and implicit signposts at different levels in the text.

Titles as Signposts

The first signpost in a dissertation is the title. As the title page is the first part of a dissertation that a potential reader will look at, it is vitally important that the title is as informative as possible. The readers will then be able to easily judge how useful the text is likely to be for them. An informative title will also make the task of a librarian cataloguing the dissertation much easier and will make a keyword search much more straightforward for anyone searching information in a particular field. Below is an example of a situation where an uninformative and misleading title was initially proposed.

EXAMPLE 5.1

A student of real estate and construction investigating the effects of a government directive to set up centres for mentally handicapped adults in residential areas chose the title:

Monetary Implications of Social Welfare Policies

This title was a very poor signpost since it was too vague and failed to reflect the contents of the dissertation. Such a title would have made it difficult for a librarian to catalogue the dissertation and, consequently, difficult for other researchers in that area to find the work. A far more informative title would have been:

The Effect on Land and Housing Prices of the Establishment of Mental Health Rehabilitation Centres in the Community

The second title gives more detail in terms of what monetary implications are being referred to and which social welfare policy is being considered. It is far more informative. In fact, the two titles above could have been combined with a colon placed between the two parts:

Monetary Implications of Social Welfare Policies: The Effect on Land and Housing Prices of the Establishment of Mental Health Rehabilitation Centres in the Community

This would create quite a long title, but it is not uncommon for a dissertation title to be broken into two parts in this way in order to provide adequate information for potential readers. There is another example on p. 133 where the part following the colon provides more information on the general area indicated before the colon.

EXAMPLE 5.2

Disruptive Students: A Case Study in a Texas Community College

This title makes it clear to the reader what kind of study to expect, what sort of students are being studied and where. You should note, however, that length does not necessarily determine how informative a title is, and a short title may work in some cases, such as the following title from a philosophy dissertation:

EXAMPLE 5.3

On Freud's Theory of the Unconscious

There is no doubt from this title which theory is being investigated and a clarifying subtitle is, therefore, unnecessary.

TASK 5.2

Look at the following titles and say whether they are adequate in terms of the information they provide. Would they help a potential reader to know what to expect in the dissertation?

1. A quantitative and qualitative analysis of the anterior dentition visible in photographs and its application to forensic odontology
2. The impact of environmental measures on the industrial areas of Singapore
3. The effect of task type on negotiation of meaning in small group work in the language class
4. Education in the People's Republic of China since 1978
5. A probabilistic approach to slope stability for Hong Kong

Subtitles as Signposts

Dissertation chapters should be broken up into sections with each of the sections being given a subtitle, sometimes referred to as a subheading. Like titles, subtitles need to be informative; they need to tell the reader as accurately as possible the theme of the text that follows, as in the example below:

EXAMPLE 5.4

Subjects

A group of 90 first-year students studying in the Faculty of Arts at the University of Hong Kong were identified for this study. They were all taking the English for Arts Students (EAS) course run by the English Centre. They were from 6 of the 40 EAS groups being taught in the academic year 1994–95. The students were identified on the basis of their availability to take part in the study, though as noted in the study in Chapter 5, students were not randomly placed into groups at the beginning of the academic year.

In the above example a single-word subtitle is sufficient; however, usually more than one word is needed for the subtitle to be informative. In the following example, taken from the first draft of a proposal to develop a new method of calculating slope stability for Hong Kong, the subtitle is too general.

EXAMPLE 5.5

Rainfall

The most noticeable feature of rainfall in Hong Kong is its very large variability from year to year. As Hong Kong lies within the circulation of a tropical cyclone, showers are usually heavy and frequent. It has been estimated that nearly a quarter of the yearly rainfall is associated with tropical cyclones, the intensity of which can be high, with 24-hour rainfall of more than 250 mm and one-hour rainfall of more than 50 mm occurring fairly frequently. The most intense rainfall is associated with thunderstorm clouds caused by low pressure. The maximum extreme rainfall ever recorded in Hong Kong was as follows:

1 year: 3060 mm	(1889)
1 month: 1240 mm	(1889)
24 hours: 697 mm	(1889)
1 hour: 157 mm	(1968)

The relationship between rainfall and landslides for Hong Kong was first established by Lumb (1975), who concluded that the magnitude of 15 days antecedent rainfall, the total rainfall of the preceding 15 days, can be used as an indicator of the likelihood of landslides.

Based on the analysis of all the times of occurrences of landslides for the 25 year period 1963–1982 [sic], more appropriate rainfall conditions associated with slope movements have been proposed by Brand (1984), who indicated that the antecedent rainfall is not a major factor in landslide occurrence. He suggested that the large majority of landslides are induced by localized short duration rainfall of high intensity.

The landslide sites in relation to isohyets of three-hour rainfall (mm) are plotted in Fig. 2 and this diagram illustrates that most landslides are located in two major rainfall areas associated with the rainstorm event. Such distributions are typical for Hong Kong.

In this example, the writer is discussing rainfall intensity and its relationship to landslides in Hong Kong, not other aspects of rainfall. A more informative subtitle would have been:

Rainfall intensity and landslides

Note:

In the text above, we have inserted [sic] after 'the period 1963–82'. This is the standard method for indicating that there is an error in the original text (1963–82 is not 25 years!). This insertion is made, in square brackets, in quoted text to make sure that *your* reader is aware that the error is *not yours*, but was in the original. Any error is indicated in this way, be it a grammar, spelling or factual error.

TASK 5.3

Read through the extracts below and suggest appropriate subtitles for each.

1. Discrimination based on psychiatric disabilities is one of the leading causes why persons file complaints with the Equal Employment Opportunity Commission (EEOC) (see Table 1). The psychiatric disabilities that are the basis for these complaints include but are not limited to anxiety disorders, depression, bipolar disorder, and schizophrenia.

    Employers at times discriminate against people with psychiatric disabilities because of popular misconceptions. These misconceptions include the beliefs that people with psychiatric disabilities are likely to be violent; that they can never recover from their mental illness; or that they cannot tolerate stress on the job. The data in Table 1 suggests that a significant number of people with psychiatric disabilities may be treated differently in the workplace given the large number of job discrimination complaints filed by this protected group.

2. The present study has a major limitation in its design. Since a true experimental design is unethical and impractical to carry out, a less exemplary method is adopted in this study. In the present study, we made an effort to match the socioeconomic background of all subjects in the two groups and hoped that this effort could somewhat limit some of the important pre-existing group differences. The major deficiency in matching strategy of quasi-experimentation is that even when it appears that we have matched perfectly on a pre-test the pre-existing group differences are likely to reappear on the post-test and make it impossible for us to decide whether the differences we observe after the intervention are the result of the intervention or are the resurgence of the pre-existing difference. Therefore, caution needs to be taken on the interpretation about the influence and benefits of the elderly health promotion program in Hong Kong.

SIGNPOSTING: HIERARCHICAL ORGANISATION OF TEXT

It is important to make clear to the readers the relationship between topics and subtopics. One way this is achieved is through varying the level of subheadings and numbering these accordingly. Where this hierarchy of text is most apparent is in the Table of Contents. In the following example from a Table of Contents, a dissertation chapter has been divided into five sections, all of which are at the same level. This can be seen not only by the numbering used, but by the indentation adopted and the choice of font styles.

EXAMPLE 5.6

Chapter 3: Consciousness and Language Acquisition
- 3.0 Overview
- 3.1 Nature of Consciousness
- 3.2 Ambiguities of Consciousness
- 3.3 The Role of Consciousness in SLA
- 3.4 Summary

This chapter could have been reorganised to show that two aspects of consciousness would be considered. This would be particularly useful if some general points about consciousness were to be made before the writer moved on to the first subtopic, the nature of consciousness.

EXAMPLE 5.7

- 3.1 Consciousness
  - 3.1.1 The nature of consciousness
  - 3.1.2 Ambiguities of consciousness
- 3.2 The role of consciousness in SLA

Such breaking up of long text into subsections is necessary to ensure clarity, but it is advisable not to introduce too many levels of subheadings as this tends to complicate rather than clarify the relationships between sections. **Four** levels are the maximum recommended for a dissertation. Example 5.8 illustrates how numbering and indentation as well as different size and styles of font can be used to best effect.

EXAMPLE 5.8: EXTRACT FROM A TABLE OF CONTENTS

The reader can immediately see from the layout of this section of the Table of Contents how the writer has subdivided the topics to indicate hierarchical relationships. In this way the Table of Contents acts as a signpost for the dissertation.

TASK 5.4

Critique the following Table of Contents from a Masters dissertation in terms of how informative it is for the reader.

Table of Contents

SIGNPOSTING WITHIN TEXT

Signposting is also used within a text to signal organisation to the reader. Words such as *first, next, then, subsequently* act as signposts or organisational markers. They signal the organisation of a text **explicitly** to the reader. In Example 5.9 the signposts have been italicised.

EXAMPLE 5.9

> *First*, we consider some variable properties of performance assessment in contradistinction to multiple choice. *Next*, we examine the tension between task-driven and construct-driven performance assessment in terms of whether the performance is to serve as the target of the vehicle of the assessment. *Then* we highlight the two major sources of test invalidity because they provide a basis for determining what "authenticity" and "directness" of performance assessment might mean in validity terms.

The reader can tell from this text exactly what will be discussed and in what order. The organisation is made clear, but using such explicit signposts too frequently within a short piece of text may prove boring for readers. The alternative is to use **implicit signposts** where the organisation of a text or section is implied by the order in which information is provided instead of by the use of specific words or phrases. The following example illustrates a text which uses implicit signposts.

EXAMPLE 5.10

> This aspect of sociological perspective can be clarified by looking at two important areas of investigation – social control and social stratification.

By mentioning social control before social stratification the writer is telling his readers that he will first consider social control and then social stratification. The organisation of the text that follows is implied in the order in which the two aspects of sociological perspective are mentioned. The organisation is signalled in the same way in the following longer example.

EXAMPLE 5.11

> Valuations and appraisals are the product of human judgement. This paper explores the contention that such judgement may incorporate elements of cognitive bias. It assumes that a clearer grasp of the

impact of such bias may assist in understanding what leads to 'inaccuracy' in valuations. It outlines the case for questioning the validity of the rational assumptions that underlie models of valuation behaviour, and focuses on one particular form of deviation from rationality: confirmation bias. It presents and discusses the results of a survey designed to test for associations of characteristics that might support the case for the presence of confirmation bias in valuer behavior. It concludes that the case for the presence of confirmation bias is unproved.

Although signposts may come at any point within a text, they are most commonly found towards the end of an introduction, whether it is the introduction to the whole dissertation or the introduction to a section or chapter. This is because they prepare readers for what will come next. (You would be well advised to refer back to Chapter 1 where this feature of the introductory chapter was considered.) Where the sole purpose of an introduction is to provide an overview of a chapter of a dissertation, the entire introduction may act as a signpost as in Example 5.12.

EXAMPLE 5.12

Chapter 5. RESULTS AND DISCUSSION

This chapter addresses the overall research question: "What is the effect of task type on negotiation of meaning?" The results of the descriptive question on length of interactions (Section 5.1) are presented first as baseline data. This is followed by an in-depth analysis of three dimensions, investigating various effects of task type on negotiation of meaning. Dimension 1, the effects of task type on opportunities for negotiation of meaning, aims to validate the five-task framework (Section 5.2) of Pica, Kanagy, and Falodun (1993). Dimension 2 considers the effects of cognitive demands of different task types on density of negotiation sequence (Section 5.3). Next Dimension 1 and 2 are combined in an analysis of the effects of task type on the use of specific exponents of repair (Section 5.4).

Section 5.5 presents Dimension 3, the effects of task type on conditions and processes of second language acquisition. A qualitative analysis of selected negotiation of meaning sequences examines how learners provide one another with the conditions necessary for second language acquisition through an integrated focus on form and meaning and illustrates language learning processes during interaction.

Each section begins with the research question(s) and, depending on the nature of the question(s) and the results, continues as follows: hypotheses, data description, statistical analysis, discussion, post hoc analysis, and summary. In each sub-section where both absolute and relative frequencies are used, the former precedes the latter.

Signposts may also act as a link between sections as in Example 5.13.

EXAMPLE 5.13

... Of course, it can be difficult to determine whether a participant in an electronic monitoring scheme is a true divertee from prison, and there are as yet no empirical data available as to net-widening in more than a couple of state and county schemes. Nevertheless, net-widening is a danger which has implications not only for those caught within the net of social control but also for the cost-effectiveness of the scheme, and the cost-effectiveness is a fundamental rationale for many electronic monitoring programmes.

Cost-effectiveness

The 1988 Green Paper revealed a perception on the part of the Government that tagging was likely to be cheaper than imprisonment
...

In this extract the notion of 'cost-effectiveness' is raised towards the end of the introduction of a journal article and then taken up in detail in the following section of the paper that is subheaded 'Cost-effectiveness'.

TASK 5.5

Read through the three extracts below and consider the following questions:

(a) What words or expressions are used in the text to signpost?

(b) Is the signposting explicit or implicit?

(c) Is the signposting adequate?

1. The aim of this paper is to demonstrate the relevance of possible-world frameworks to the study of poetic text worlds. My argument will proceed as follows. In the first part of the paper, I will briefly discuss the development of the notion of possible worlds from logic to the semantics of fictionality, and consider the way in which a possible-world approach can be used to describe and classify fictional worlds; I will focus particularly on the framework developed by Ryan (1991a, 1991b). In the second part of the paper, I will show how possible-world models, and specifically Ryan's approach, can be applied to poetry. In particular, I will adopt a possible-world perspective in order to consider:

   i.   the internal structure of the world projected by a particular poem;

   ii.   the projection of deviant situations of address;

   iii. the description of different types of poetic worlds.

   I will conclude with a discussion of the main weaknesses of possible-world frameworks, and with some suggestions for future developments in the study of text worlds.

2. The next section of this paper describes the housing policy situation in a number of Latin American countries, including Bolivia, to provide some comparative contexts for the FONVIS program. The following section details the low-income urban housing situation in Bolivia with emphasis on the largest cities, i.e. La Paz, El Alto, and Santa Cruz (figure 1). Next, the FONVIS program and its achievements up to and including 1994 are described, while the following section outlines the shortcomings

of the organization's approach. Finally, the paper concludes with specific recommendations regarding how the FONVIS program might be modified to actually address the needs of those without access to housing credit.

3. This paper explores the association between type of contract and job satisfaction and stress levels by studying the introduction of salaried contracts in the UK. In the first section we develop simple hypotheses to be tested using descriptive information on salaried contracts in PMS pilots. In the empirical section we use data from two surveys to compare job satisfaction and stress levels of GPs on salaried contracts with GPs on the standard GMS contract. A secondary comparison is made to establish whether job satisfaction is higher in PMS pilot sites more generally by comparing GPs on salaried contract with their PMS GP employers (referred to as non-salaried PMS GPs).

SUMMARIES AS SIGNPOSTS

Signposts are also frequently found in the form of chapter and section summaries. Their function is somewhat different to that discussed earlier in that they remind readers of where they have been rather than tell readers where they are going. Example 5.14 shows how a summary is used to tie together what was said earlier and to highlight what the writer considered to be the most salient points.

EXAMPLE 5.14

In summary, linguistic features were the most frequently noted in this study and of these, pace was the single most important characteristic for both NSs [native speakers] and NNSs [non-native speakers] alike. However, it was not noted with equal consistency for all texts. Where pace was noted by the respondents, it appears to have been more dependent on the professionalism of the speakers than the authenticity of the extracts. Furthermore, the identification of text characteristics did not always lead to correct decisions regarding text authenticity. The slow pace of the lecturer in text 14(A), for example, led 28 respondents to classify this text incorrectly as developed for testing purposes.

Summaries are very important in dissertation writing and their usefulness in tying ideas together and drawing attention to salient points should not be overlooked. Summaries help readers through the complex ideas that are being presented and ensure that readers do not lose their way as they proceed on their journey. It should be noted also that summaries do not only appear at the end of chapters, but may appear at the end of large sections, particularly in the literature review covering several different themes.

TASK 5.6

Read through the following summaries and decide what was being discussed in more detail earlier in the text.

1. In sum, a theory and model of African American drug use needs to adjust to the heterogeneity of a society in schism, the alternative economic functions served by drugs, and both the perceived and actual exclusion of segments of inner-city African Americans from the opportunity structure.

2. In summary, the most important findings of our study were that subjective QoL [quality of life] of first contact patients differs clearly from the QoL of long-term patients. Illness severity among 'overall users' was rated highest, but they did not assess their QoL as low as expected. They probably adapted to circumstances of living and illness severity. Furthermore, de-institutionalisation improves QoL and OLS [overall life satisfaction] is mainly predicted by subjective variables.

SIGNPOSTING: LANGUAGE FEATURES

It is quite common in English for an inanimate subject, such as 'article', 'paper', 'chapter', and 'study', to be followed by an active (not passive) verb. This is illustrated in Example 5.15 where the active verbs are italicised.

EXAMPLE 5.15

The next section of this paper *describes* the housing policy situation in a number of Latin American countries, including Bolivia, to provide some comparative contexts for the FONVIS program. [1] The following section *details* the low-income urban housing situation in Bolivia with emphasis on the largest cities, i.e. La Paz, El Alto, and Santa Cruz (figure 1). [2] Next, the FONVIS program and its achievements up to and including 1994 are described, while the following section *outlines* the shortcomings of the organization's approach. [3] Finally, the paper *concludes* with specific recommendations regarding how the FONVIS program might be modified to actually address the needs of those without access to housing credit. [4]

In Sentences 1 and 4, the subject of the sentence is 'paper'. In theory a paper cannot 'describe' or 'conclude' anything — it is the authors who do the describing and concluding, but inherent in the nature of this subject is the implied human agent. Hence, the active verb form is not only allowed, but preferred. The same is true for Sentence 2 and the second part of Sentence 3 where the subject is 'the following section [of the paper]'. However, in the first part of Sentence 3 where the subject is 'the FONVIS program and its achievements' the verb is in the passive as it is not inherent in the nature of 'achievements' to describe anything.

Nouns which imply a human agent and regularly take the active voice in academic writing include: results, data, figure, research, profile, model, table, paper, dissertation, work, and chapter.

There are two other categories of inanimate or abstract nouns which take active forms of verbs in academic writing. These are:

- nominalised verbs (nouns that come from a verb) such as *analysis*, *comparison*, and *measurement*;
- items of equipment, such as *thermometer* and *lens*.

EXAMPLE 5.16

The results demonstrate ...
The dissertation considers ...
The data show ...
The analysis suggests ...
This comparison clearly indicates ...
The measurement includes ...
The thermometer reads ...
The lens focuses ...

TASK 5.7

Identify the inanimate or abstract nouns in the extracts below. Then decide whether they are followed by a verb in the active or passive form. Which section of a paper do you think each of the extracts has been taken from?

1. Findings of this study support the observations of Cobb et al. (1999), Garcia (1985), Gitomer et al. (1999), and Hicken (1992) that the percentage of minority students who do not achieve passing scores on basic skills teacher competency tests is disproportionately higher than the percentage of White students who do not pass. Data in table 5 show that over 44.4% of African American preservice teachers and 29.8% of Hispanic preservice teachers initially failed one or more of the PPST subtests, compared with only 11.1% of White students.

2. The argument has three parts. The first is a discussion of the constraints on Liberal legislators in 1906. It suggests that the

government had more room for manoeuvre than has sometimes been suggested and does so by examining the legal background, the position of trade unions in popular affections, and the legacy of the general election. The second examines the meaning of the debate both in and out of Parliament. It aims to put the Act in its proper intellectual context by attending to the variety of views about trade union law extant in Edwardian liberalism. The final section reassesses the passage of the Act and its implications for our understanding of the character of Liberalism and the Liberal Party as it took up the reins of government for the last time.

Bringing It All Together

Signposts are organisational markers which help readers through a text.

- ❖ Signposts take the form of:
  - titles;
  - subtitles/subheadings;
  - markers within the text.
- ❖ Titles and subtitles are only useful if they are informative.
- ❖ The relationship between topics and subtopics is indicated through the use of different levels of subheadings.
- ❖ Within the text signposts may be explicit or implicit.
- ❖ Too many explicit signposts within a short stretch of text may be boring.
- ❖ Forward-looking signposts inform readers of what will come in succeeding text.
- ❖ Backward-looking signposts remind readers of what has been said earlier.
- ❖ Signposts occur most frequently towards the end of an introduction, chapter or section.

Signposting in Academic Papers

Signposting is equally important in academic papers and book chapters as evidenced from many of the examples in this chapter. However, the title of a journal article or book chapter does not necessarily have to be as informative as in a dissertation. Anyone reaching for a journal is likely to know what broad area the journal covers and, therefore, the writer may want to attract readers' attention to the article by using an interesting title as in the examples below:

> **Why the 'Monkey Passage' Bombed: Tests, Genres and Teaching**
>
> (A paper published in *Harvard Education Review,* 1995)
>
> **Hamlet Without the Prince: Structural Adjustment, Firm Behaviour and Private Investment**
>
> (A book chapter in *Finance Development and Structural Change,* edited by Arestis, Philip and Victoria Chick, 1995)

As academic journals differ in their submission requirements, it is always advisable to check the specifications before making a submission. Many limit the number of levels of subheadings that may be used. They may also specify the font size and placing of the subheadings within the text.

As articles are limited in length, there is much less necessity to include a summary in the body of the text.

Further Advice

As you read through academic papers in your field, look specifically for signposts. Ask yourself how well the abstracts signpost the content and whether the headings and subheadings help you understand the text. Check the location and use of signposts within the text. Note whether they are explicit or implicit. You need to adapt a style of signposting which is consistent with the style used in your discipline or any particular journal to which you submit papers for publication.

Follow-up Tasks

1. Look at the Table of Contents in two or three dissertations and then take one chapter from each dissertation and see if it is possible to predict the content of the subsections from the subtitles.
2. Imagine that you have been asked by the Postgraduate Society of your university to write a short piece on your research for the society's newsletter. Write a paper of approximately 300 words, bearing in mind that your audience are staff and students who are not necessarily in your field. Pay particular attention to your language and to helping your readers through the text by using appropriate signposts.

6 The Final Touches

As you are writing your dissertation, you will need to keep proofreading and editing your text to ensure that it is easy to follow and error-free. You will also need to read it through one final time before you submit your dissertation. We should at this point distinguish between proofreading and editing. The former refers to the process of reading a text to detect surface errors, such as spelling mistakes or missing plurals. These errors, although they are extremely irritating to a reader and give an impression of carelessness, do not generally impede understanding of the text, unless they are overly abundant. Editing, on the other hand, involves careful reading to ensure that the text runs smoothly enough to be readily understood by a reader without undue effort and with no possible ambiguities of meaning. Editing a text may involve quite substantial rewriting, unlike the quick additions and deletions you make while proofreading. This last chapter of the book will now look at certain features of text that you should consider when editing your writing as they will make your work easier to read.

CREATING COHESIVE TEXT

If, on rereading your text yourself, you find that your message seems unclear, or if you receive feedback from your supervisor saying that certain parts are difficult to follow, you may need to consider how cohesive your text is. The cohesion of a text, that is to say, the way the sentences in the text are tied together and follow on smoothly from each other, is achieved to some extent by grammatical accuracy, such as the use of the correct tense. This is one aspect of your writing that you may need to improve and we have discussed the appropriate tense to use at several points throughout the book, but it is beyond our scope to cover general grammar constructions in detail. Cohesion is also achieved, however, by the order in which the information given in each sentence is presented and by the correct use of vocabulary and pronoun reference. It is these three aspects of cohesion that we will consider in the following sections.

COHESIVE TEXT: INFORMATION STRUCTURE

When we talk of information structure in a language, this is referring to the order in which the information given in each sentence is presented. The order of presentation has a great impact on the readability of a text, that is to say, the ease with which a text can be understood. To see how information structure works in English, we can study the different ways the statements given below can be combined into continuous text as an example.

Statements

Here are 23 statements of facts or ideas about language teaching which can be used to form the introductory paragraph(s) to a textbook for teachers.

1. There is a pendulum effect in language teaching.
2. Overcoming the pendulum effect is an important task.
3. Applied linguists confront this task.
4. Teachers who are concerned with foreign language learning confront this task.
5. Teachers who are concerned with second language learning confront this task.
6. The pendulum effect is most evident in the area of methodology.

7. In the area of methodology, fads and fashions come and go.

8. Fads and fashions come and go with monotonous regularity.

9. Fads and fashions are like theories of grammar in this regard.

10. There is a way to overcome the pendulum effect.

11. The way to overcome the pendulum effect is to derive effective classroom practices from empirical evidence.

12. The empirical evidence should relate to the nature of language learning.

13. The empirical evidence should relate to the nature of language use.

14. Effective classroom practices should also be derived from insights into what makes learners tick.

15. This book has a major purpose.

16. The major purpose is to introduce teachers to an empirically based approach to language teaching methodology.

17. The book also aims to introduce teachers in preparation to an empirically based approach to language teaching methodology.

18. An empirically based approach integrates theory and research with insights.

19. The theory and research relate to the nature of language learning and use.

20. The insights are derived from observation of what actually goes on in classrooms.

21. The insights are also derived from analysis of what actually goes on in classrooms.

22. What actually goes on in classrooms is often opposed to what some say should go on.

23. An empirically based approach uses the knowledge gained from the classroom to inform the issues that are raised and the points that are made.

These statements could be combined in a variety of ways to make a continuous text. The first step in combining the ideas is to consider which ideas are so closely connected that they could be grouped together into each sentence of a text. If we do this with the 23 statements above, we find that the following combinations are strongly indicated:

Statements	1–5
Statements	6–9
Statements	10–14
Statements	15–17
Statements	18–23

Below are two possible versions of a paragraph combining the ideas from each group of statements.

Complete paragraph: Version A

Overcoming the pendulum effect in language teaching is an important task confronting applied linguists and teachers concerned with second and foreign language learning. [1] Methodology is the area where the pendulum effect is most evident because it is in methodology that fads and fashions, like theories of grammar, come and go with monotonous regularity. [2] Deriving appropriate classroom practices from empirical evidence on the nature of language learning and use and from insights into what makes learners tick is the way to overcome the pendulum effect. [3] To introduce teachers and teachers in preparation to an empirically based approach to language teaching methodology is the major purpose of this book. [4] The knowledge gained from integrating theory and research into the nature of language learning and use with insights derived from the observation and analysis of what actually goes on in classrooms (as opposed to what some say should go on) is used to inform the issues raised and points made. [5]

Complete paragraph: Version B

An important task confronting applied linguists and teachers concerned with second and foreign language learning is to overcome the pendulum effect in language teaching. [1] This effect is most evident in the area of methodology where fads and fashions, like theories of grammar, come and go with monotonous regularity. [2] The way to overcome the pendulum effect is to derive appropriate classroom practices from empirical evidence on the nature of language learning and use and from insights into what makes learners tick. [3] Language teaching methodology is the focus of this book, the major purpose of which is to introduce teachers and teachers in preparation to an empirically based approach to methodology. [4] Such an approach integrates theory and research into the nature of language learning and use, with insights derived from the observation and analysis of what actually goes on in classrooms (as opposed to what some say should go on), and uses this knowledge to inform the issues raised and points made. [5]

Both paragraphs are equally coherent, that is to say, the message in each can be understood, but Version B is more cohesive; it is easier for a reader to follow. Given that each sentence contains the same information, we need to look at how the order in which the information is presented affects the ease of understanding the text. What we can notice is that each sentence in **Version A**, after the first one, begins with a new term that has not previously been mentioned in the text:

Sentence 2	*Methodology*
Sentence 3	*Deriving appropriate classroom practices from empirical evidence*
Sentence 4	*To introduce teachers and teachers in preparation*
Sentence 5	*The knowledge gained from integrating theory and research*

However in **Version B,** each sentence, after the first one, begins with a reference to an aspect that has been mentioned earlier in the text, although not necessarily in the immediately preceding sentence.

Sentence 2	*This effect* (referring back to *the pendulum effect*)
Sentence 3	*The way to overcome the pendulum effect* (referring back to *the pendulum effect*)
Sentence 4	*Language teaching methodology* (referring back to *methodology*, Sentence 2)
Sentence 5	*Such an approach* (referring back to *an empirically based approach*, Sentence 4)

It is this aspect of continuous text in academic English that helps to create cohesion. Each sentence begins with a backward reference, rather than a new term. This type of organisation is referred to as 'given-new' information structure. It complies with the convention in English of sentences having 'end focus'; that is to say, the main point of a sentence comes towards the end, or to be more precise, after the main verb, while the first part of the sentence, before the main verb, acts as a connection to the earlier text. Of course not all text is constructed so precisely; literary works often do not follow these conventions closely at all. However, as this type of sentence organisation is common in academic writing because it leads to greater clarity and makes text more easily readable, it is one feature of your text that you should look at if the message you are trying to convey is not clear.

TASK 6.1

Read the following text, which is the opening paragraph to an article in a geography journal, and consider if the sentences follow a given-new information structure. For each sentence that follows this structure, decide what aspect of the preceding text is being referred to and by which reference item.

Coming into the 1990s, the environment of investment in China has changed from the 80s when a large amount of small export-oriented joint ventures (JV) mainly invested by Newly Industrialized Economies (NIES) prevailed and were geographically concentrated in coastal regions. [1] Under the new environment, foreign investors are encouraged by a variety of incentive measures, to diversify their investments in space and toward some "bottlenecked" industries and sectors of the economy. [2] Such a change, as to be argued by this paper, is attributed mainly to three parallel processes. [3] The first process is the changing degree of openness for foreign investments in space and by sectors deliberately and gradually set by the central government. [4] The second process is a decentralization of power, which has allowed local governments and enterprises to be more independent in introducing foreign investment as well as in organizing their economy. [5] Industrial restructuring is the third process, which has been reshaping China's industry in two major ways. [6] One way is to build up a mix of ownership with more and more collective and private firms in place of a structure of state-ownership domination. [7] The other way is to formulate a more market-oriented institutional structure, linking the ministries, provincial governments, and enterprises in a flexible, multi-channel manner so that individual enterprises as well as the government at the lower level may respond faster to the market needs. [8] As a consequence of such restructuring, the firms are becoming more competitive while less likely to follow the central planning commands positively when interests conflict. [9] The new institutional structure is also reforming the channels of financial and material flows among the parties involved. [10] In between the central government and enterprises, local governments may behave differently in responding to many foreign investment issues. [11]

COHESIVE TEXT: VOCABULARY CHOICE

The cohesion of a text is also achieved to some extent by your vocabulary choices. The words you choose and where you place them contribute considerably to the readability of your writing. To see how this works, let us study the text below, which is an extract from an MPhil dissertation in dentistry, reporting on how photographs of front teeth could be used in forensic odontology.

EXAMPLE 6.1

For the first time in legal history, in the case of the *Crown v Lam* (High Court of Hong Kong 1983) – the so-called Jar Murders – identification of the victims by photographic superimposition was acceptable. [1] In one instance, the separation between the cusps of the upper canine teeth of a postmortem dentition was used to establish the enlargement of the antemortem photographs in which these teeth were visible. [2] When life-sized transparencies of the skull and the antemortem photographs were superimposed, an accurate correspondence between the features of the anterior dentition seen in them was established. [3] Three murder victims, none of whom had useful dental records, were identified in this way. [4] A legal precedent was created in the High Court of Hong Kong when the identification of these victims was accepted not only by the Coroner, but also by both the prosecution and defence counsels.

Because this text is combining three themes, **the law**, **photography** and **dentistry**, we can, naturally, expect to find vocabulary related to these three word families. It is important to note, however, how the words related to these three families are distributed. If we look at Table 6.1 below,

Table 6.1   Vocabulary ties

	LAW	PHOTOGRAPHY	DENTISTRY
Sentence 1	legal case Crown High Court Murders victims	photographic	
Sentence 2		photographs	cusps canine teeth dentition
Sentence 3		photographs	dentition
Sentence 4	murder victims		dental
Sentence 5	legal High Court victims Coroner prosecution defence counsels		

we can see that each sentence, apart from the concluding one of the paragraph, which does not need to connect with a following sentence, deals with two of the three themes.

This use of related vocabulary across sentence boundaries helps to tie text together. We do not have a series of separate sentences, each one dealing with one of the themes. This use of vocabulary complies with the use of given-new information structure, where each sentence refers back to part of the text that has gone before.

We should also notice that vocabulary other than that connected to the themes of the text plays a role in tying the text together. There are a number of word roots (not connected to the law, photography and dentistry) which are repeated throughout the paragraph. These are shown in Table 6.2 below:

Table 6.2   Using word roots for cohesion

VOCABULARY ITEM	SENTENCE
identification	1 & 5
identified	4
superimposition	1
superimposed	3
acceptable	1
accepted	5
establish	2
established	3
antemortem	2 & 3
postmortem	2
used	2
useful	4

The repetition of the root of a word, *across*, rather than *within* sentences is one device whereby the cohesion of a text is enhanced as the repetition of a root causes the reader's mind to refer back to the last time that root was used.

TASK 6.2

Look through a piece of your own writing, concentrating on your use of vocabulary, and consider if the cohesion of your writing could be improved by repetition of words or word roots *across* sentence boundaries.

COHESIVE TEXT: MORE ON VOCABULARY

Use of Synonyms

Writers do not always use the same expression to refer to the same idea; they sometimes deliberately vary their choice of vocabulary to avoid sounding monotonous by repeating the same word or expression too frequently, particularly in informal or literary texts. However, synonyms must be used with caution in academic writing as many words do not have an exact synonym; using two different words to refer to the same concept may change the meaning slightly. Caution should also be exercised when using a thesaurus to look for synonyms as two words may be synonymous in one context but not so in another.

Sentence Connectors

It is a common misconception that cohesion can be created in a text by frequent use of connecting devices, such as 'besides', 'moreover' and 'thus', across sentences. These devices do, of course, have their place in signalling relationships, but they are no more than overt signals of relationships that already exist; they do not create a relationship between sentences and their overuse is very uncharacteristic of well-written English text. In fact, when they are overused they become obtrusive. If we look at the text from the geography journal in Task 6.1 above, for example, we can see only one instance of a sentence connector — 'also' in Sentence 10.

EXAMPLE 6.2

As a consequence of such restructuring, the firms are becoming more competitive while less likely to follow the central planning commands positively when interests conflict. [9] The new institutional structure is *also* reforming the channels of financial and material flows among the parties involved. [10]

Table 6.3 below shows the frequency of the most common sentence connectors according to the LOB (London-Oslo/Bergen) corpus, which surveyed 1 million words in written English. We can note from the list that the only connectors used with any regularity are 'also', 'however' and 'therefore'. These three words allow a writer to indicate the three main relationships between ideas that need to be shown, that is **addition** ('also'), **contrast** ('however') and **result** ('therefore'). Other connectors can be used on occasion for the sake of variety, but, if given–new information structure is adhered to, sentence connectors are often not needed at all and their overuse should be avoided.

Table 6.3   Connectives

CONNECTIVE	Number of uses per million words
Also	994
However	566
Therefore	296
Nevertheless	92
Moreover	55
Consequently	44
Besides	42
Furthermore	25

NB.   The LOB study did not consider clause connectors *within* sentences, i.e. 'and', 'but', 'so'.

Note:

'Also' may appear to have an extraordinarily high usage, but this is probably because, unlike 'however' and 'therefore', it can be used to join elements within a clause as well as to join sentences and the LOB study measured only the presence of these connectors in texts, not their function.

Another point to note with relation to connectives is that they are not always sentence initial. If we look at the use of 'also' in Sentence 10 of the text in Task 6.1, we can see that the connective does not come at the beginning of the sentence; it comes after the subject of the sentence and between the auxiliary and main part of the verb.

EXAMPLE 6.3

The new institutional structure is also reforming … .

It is very common for sentence connectors to appear in this position, or they may come after the verb 'to be' or after the subject of the sentence. We can see connectors used in all three positions in the examples below:

EXAMPLE 6.4

The constitution prohibits extension of a president's time in office beyond two consecutive terms. The present incumbent, *therefore*, is ineligible for re-election.

EXAMPLE 6.5

The constitution prohibits extension of a president's time in office beyond two consecutive terms. The present incumbent is, *however*, seeking to have this clause overturned.

EXAMPLE 6.6

The constitution prohibits extension of a president's time in office beyond two consecutive terms. There is *also* a prohibition against any past president running for office for a third time within a period of 10 years.

TASK 6.3

Look at the following text on transport problems in Hong Kong. This text was written by a student and it contains a number of redundant sentence connectors. Decide which connectives could be omitted. Aside from leaving out some of the connectives, are there any other changes you could make to improve this piece of writing?

First of all, traffic congestion is most serious in Hong Kong, especially during rush hours around 7.00 to 9.00 in the morning and 5.00 to 7.30 in the afternoon. Moreover, there is also significant spatial variations. Congestion is especially terrible in various spots during peak hours, e.g. the entrance of the Cross Harbour Tunnel, in Central district and Tsing Yi Bridge. Besides, the narrowness of streets also contributes to the traffic congestion, e.g. Caine Road.

Secondly, there is a great dependence on public transport modes such as buses, trains and subways. In recent years, there has been a great increase in demand. However, increase in the intensity of demand is greater relative to the spread of demand. About 80% of the total demand for public transport is confined to a mere 20 hours of the week. During rush hours each day, all the public transport facilities are fully utilized. But at other times public transport suffers from the problem of too few passengers. Then the bus companies tend to cut down the numbers of buses in order to lessen the operating costs. However, this leads to inconvenience for people because the waiting time for buses is increased.

Thirdly, parking deficiency is another transport problem in Hong Kong. With the high density of buildings and narrow streets, there are very few possible places to park. Consequently, even with low levels of car ownership, the streets and often the footpaths are choked with parked vehicles. For example, Garden Road in Central District is narrow and steep and has a sharp turn. However, many cars are parked along this road. Thus, drivers have to be very careful in turning the sharp corner and this is very dangerous.

Cohesive Text: Pronoun Reference

One other factor that can undermine the cohesion of a text is the misuse of pronouns. A pronoun can only be used to replace a noun if its reference is immediately clear and unambiguous. The use of an incorrect pronoun can seriously confuse a reader. The following example illustrates this point.

EXAMPLE 6.7

> Indira Ghandi took over as leader of the party in that year. He became a figure renowned worldwide for ruling the country with a firm, yet fair, hand.

As Indira Ghandi was a famous Indian politician in the mid-twentieth century, and was, indeed, known throughout the world, a reader looking at this sentence in the later part of that century is likely to realise, fairly quickly, that the writer has chosen the wrong pronoun to refer to Ms Ghandi. However, on seeing the pronoun referring to a person of the male gender, a reader will, initially, pause in confusion. You must remember that it is not a reader's job to reconstruct the text for the writer, guessing what it was that the writer wanted to say. What is more, there is no guarantee that at some time in the future, a reader who is no longer aware of Indira Ghandi's fame and who does not come from an Indian cultural background will know that 'Indira' is a woman's name. Such a reader would be led to believe, from the use of the pronoun *he* that Indira Ghandi was a man!

Example 6.8 below shows another instance where the use of the wrong pronoun gives misleading information.

EXAMPLE 6.8

> The positron is the antiparticle of the electron and it was discovered by Dirac.

What this sentence tells the readers is that Dirac discovered the positron, i.e. the *it* of the second clause. However, what the writer wanted to tell the readers was that Dirac discovered *the relationship between* the positron and the electron; the pronoun that should have been used was *this*. The use of an incorrect pronoun has caused readers to be misled. The misuse of the pronouns *it* and *this* in particular is the source of many misunderstandings.

TASK 6.4

Look at the pairs of sentences below and decide whether the italicised pronouns are correctly used or not. Where the pronoun is used incorrectly, what correction would you make?

1. The words used by psychologists are a constant source of anxiety to them. *They* also cause rage to their readers (including other psychologists). If *they* coin a new term, they may be accused of creating ugly and unnecessary neologisms.

2. If the open-area is larger than 3, filtration efficiency reaches a plateau, or *it* declines as *it* gets smaller.

3. The proposal is to build a small shopping centre with specialised goods to sell. *It* doesn't imply that only one item is sold, but that the shops focus on a particular group of customers.

4. The Public Utilities Regulatory Policy Act (PURPA) required regulated electric utilities to buy electricity from independent cogenerators at the 'avoided cost' of having to construct additional capacity. *This* spawned the independent power production (IPP) market in the United States.

5. COD removal efficiency in the second stage was little higher than that in the first stage. *It* was mainly due to the higher influent COD concentration.

6. The government seems to be on the point of collapse. *It* is because several scandals involving leading figures have surfaced in recent weeks.

7. I am particularly interested in examining the reasons why people speak differently in different social contexts, how the social functions of language are realised and how language is used to convey meaning. *These* will enable me to develop a deeper understanding of the problems that students face when learning a new language.

STYLISTIC FACTORS TO CONSIDER

When editing your dissertation, you must remember, as we have constantly stressed throughout this book, that what you are writing is in an *academic style*. Much of what we have said would not be appropriate to other genres of writing, works of literature or journalism, for example. Clarity is the key word in academic text and there are two factors that have an immense impact upon the clarity of your writing that you should carefully consider when editing your dissertation: the length of sentences and the length of paragraphs. We will finish our book here by considering these two factors briefly.

Paragraph Length

While there is no such thing as an ideal length for a paragraph, you should remember that in academic English the purpose of paragraph divisions is to signal a change of topic/focus. A paragraph is meant to *develop* an idea, not to merely state one fact. For this reason it is not generally possible to have a one-sentence paragraph. Use of such 'paragraphs' makes your writing look journalistic, as this technique is quite common in newspapers and magazines. It may also be used in literary texts to create a particular effect, i.e. to draw special attention to that sentence. It may be possible, in rare circumstances, in a dissertation to have a sentence which stands alone to function as a paragraph, but, in general it is not possible to develop any idea in just one sentence and, therefore, it is advisable to avoid using this technique.

Sentence Length and Complexity

We cannot, of course, claim for a sentence, any more than for a paragraph, that there is an optimum length. One sentence could be 3 words long, whilst another could be 45 words long, and both could be well-formed. It is, however, necessary to be quite a master of the language to be able to manipulate words and clauses satisfactorily to create a long and complex sentence competently. If you have difficulty in managing complex sentences without losing track of grammatical accuracy, in the interests of clarity, it is far better to write two or three shorter and less complex sentences than one long complex one. It is perfectly possible to express complex ideas in a series of simple sentences; simple sentences do not imply simple thought processes or simplistic ideas. However, it is unwise to make all your sentences short and simple as this would begin to sound monotonous for the reader; ideally you should aim to vary both the length and complexity of the sentences within a text to create a livelier style.

TASK 6.5

Look at the last sentence of Paragraph B (reproduced below), which you studied earlier in this chapter in the section on *information structure*. The sentence is rather long and complex; it would be easier to read and understand if it was split up into shorter sentences. Try to rewrite this sentence as two or three shorter sentences.

… Such an approach integrates theory and research into the nature of language learning and use, with insights derived from the observation and analysis of what actually goes on in classrooms (as opposed to what some say should go on), and uses this knowledge to inform the issues raised and points made.

CHECKLIST

Below is a list of questions that you might find useful to ask yourself when you are editing your writing.

Topic Development

Is the central topic of each paragraph readily identifiable?
Is the central topic of the paragraph fully developed within the paragraph?
Do all the sentences within a paragraph relate to the central theme or topic?

Cohesion

Are the relationships between ideas across sentences clear?
Are pronoun references correct and unambiguous?
Have ideas been 'tied together' using given-new information structure?
Does the choice of vocabulary help tie text together?
Do you rely too heavily on sentence connectors?

Clause Structure

Do main clauses carry the important information?
Has information been well combined (coordinated, subordinated) within sentences?

Grammatical Choices

Have you used the active and passive voice appropriately?
Have you clearly distinguished between ongoing and completed events as well as habitual and one-off occurrences through the appropriate use of tenses?

Vocabulary

Do you show an awareness of subject-specific vocabulary?
Is non-subject-specific vocabulary correctly used?

Proofreading

Has the document been carefully proofread?
Are there missing 's'es on third person singular verbs?
Are there missing 's'es on plurals?
Are past and present participles (*-ed* and *-ing*) used correctly?
Are adjectives and adverbs confused?
Has the document been spell-checked?
Is the spacing before and after punctuation marks correct and consistent?
Is the reference list (and/or bibliography) complete and consistently presented?
Are all quotations correctly punctuated and acknowledged with page numbers?

Bringing It All Together

There are a number of features that will enhance the readability of your text. These include:

❖ conforming to given-new information structure;
❖ choosing your vocabulary carefully;
❖ repeating word roots across sentence boundaries;
❖ avoiding overuse of sentence connectors;
❖ choosing the correct pronoun to refer back to an earlier word or idea.

Remember:

Editing and proofreading your text continuously as you are writing your dissertation will make the final task of editing much easier.

Follow-up Task

To work on improving the cohesion of your writing, go through any extended text that you have recently written and check whether you have considered all the questions in the checklist in this chapter.

Answer Key

Chapter 1

Task 1.1

Step 1: Sentence 1
Step 2: Sentences 2–5
Step 3: Sentence 6
Step 4: Sentence 11

Task 1.2

comprehensive/detailed
in-depth, not superficial
focussed on the important issues
organised thematically
analytical
critical
up-to-date
claims supported with evidence from sources
accurate in-text citations matching the list of references
provides regular summaries highlighting important information
serves as a basis to identify the research gap

Task 1.3

Text 1:   2.1   Bone formation

2.2   Bone remodeling

2.3   A mouse model with progressive hyperostosis

Text 2:   2.1   Approaches to style analysis

2.2   Uses and applications of style analysis

2.3   Property price indices

2.4   Objectives and hypotheses

Task 1.4

Text 1:   Q1:   Data is not available for prepubescent girls as a group separate from boys.

Q2:   The researchers will investigate the effects of exercise training on aerobic and anaerobic performance of prepubescent girls.

Q3:   They point out that there are significant differences between prepubescent boys and girls in aerobic and anaerobic *performance*. Therefore one might expect differences in response.

Text 2:   Q1:   Style analysis is rarely carried out in the field of real estate and, when attempted, is restricted to property funds only.

Q2:   They will investigate whether style analysis can be applied to property companies also.

Q3:   They argue that property companies and property funds have similar characteristics. (Therefore, one would expect style analysis to be applicable to companies also.)

Q4:   It identifies what it is necessary to do in order to carry out the research. It also justifies the approaches used in the research as they are the ones most favoured in the literature.

Task 1.5

(i)   Yes.

(ii)   Yes, but it has been set as a null hypothesis, indicating that there is no difference between implied and actual property allocations. It could be set as a directional hypothesis indicating that either implied property allocations are greater than or less than actual property allocations. Whether set as a directional or null hypothesis, 'should' is incorrect.

(iii) Yes.

(iv) Yes.

Task 1.6

Question: What are the effects of exercise training on the aerobic and anaerobic performance of prepubescent girls?

It is unlikely that a hypothesis would have been tested as no boys were involved in this particular study to be able to consider the difference between the response of boys and girls to aerobic and anaerobic training. Moreover, the authors acknowledge that there is sparse data available in this area, so there would be little evidence from previous research to base a hypothesis upon.

Chapter 2

Task 2.1

Extract 1

Ozanne and Murdoch (1990)   Both citations refer to criticisms
Dennis (1988)   of previous research, which lends support to the method selected in the current study. The method was, in fact, suggested by Dennis.

Extract 2

Final four lines of the text starting 'Appleton et al. 1990' in brackets. These citations support the earlier statement 'Such a decline in intellectual ability has frequently been documented ...' The numerous citations lend support to the fact that this has indeed been frequent.

Extract 3

Caplan and Hildebrandt (1988) and Kay et al. (1992) are mentioned to suggest specific examples of assessment tools used by other researchers, which might be better than the measures they used in their own research. (It is generally a good idea to suggest specific improvements, if possible, rather than to make a vague suggestion of 'using other measures'.)

Extract 4

Bruce (1983) and Hudson et al. (1989) are used to show familiarity with the field as a means of supporting the authors' findings/conclusion.

Task 2.2

Extract 1

Reporting verb	Meaning conveyed by the verb
have speculated	The writers indicate that there have been no empirical investigations, only unsupported ideas.
have … investigated	The writers neutrally report the existence of a few empirical studies, giving no indication of a positive or negative attitude towards them.
asserted	The original researcher (Kent) is reported as being very certain that his/her findings were correct.
found	The writers are reporting on a single completed study and are quite neutral about the findings; one study does not necessarily provide proof.
acknowledge	The writers indicate that other researchers recognise the situations. *Acknowledge* **can** indicate that acceptance of something was reluctant, but there is no indication of that here.

Extract 2

Reporting verb	Meaning conveyed by the verb
have been studied	The writers are reporting neutrally on the work in the field.
showed	The writers seem to be convinced by Matrix's study.
attempted to link	The writers imply that Fox failed to achieve his objective.

Task 2.3

(a) Alphabetical.
(b) No. The bracketed list of citations at the end of Extract 1 has a sequencing error: *Saegert, et al., 1980* should come after *Rocke, et al., 1980*.
(c) According to date, starting with the earliest published work.
(d) Compare.
(e) No. There is only 1 full stop at the end. It should be 'cf.' as this is short for the Latin word 'confer'.
(f) Where there are three or more authors; 'et al.' is from the Latin *et alii* meaning 'and others'. This abbreviation is used in the text only, not in the reference list.
(g) No. There should not be a comma between the first author's name and the 'et al.'. However, the punctuation of 'et al.' itself is correct; there is a full stop after 'al' to show that this is an abbreviation.

Task 2.4

Text 1		Text 2	
(1)	have suggested*	(6)	has demonstrated
(2)	tested	(7)	have relied on
(3)	observed	(8)	showed
(4)	was shown	(9)	have provided
(5)	concluded*	(10)	created
		(11)	suggested
		(12)	demonstrated

* In terms of meaning this could be changed around, but it is more usual to begin by indicating what the studies *suggested*, and end by what was *concluded*, to mirror the research process. However, as can be seen Text 2, that is not always done.

Task 2.5

This passage comes from the literature review — leading up to the identification of the research gap by the author.

Hedges used in the extract:
1. It *seems* that the results of these studies gave a false image that Elyzol dental gel can be used in the initial therapy or to replace the subgingival scaling.
2. Moreover, the study groups in the studies *seem* to have been poorly defined.

These hedges are used by the author to tone down his criticism by acknowledging that **he** may have misinterpreted the results and they could be other than they *seem*.

3. In order to define the subject groups better, subjects should *perhaps* be periodontally untreated patients ...
4. ... smokers were included in the analysis of data which *may* have affected the results of this study.

These hedges are used to stress that the writer is only making suggestions; he is not claiming to have the only possible answer.

Chapter 3

Task 3.1

1. Discussion
2. Results
3. Discussion
4. Results
5. Discussion
6. Results
7. Results
8. Discussion
9. Results

Task 3.2

Further examples of hedging devices include:

Hedging verbs: appear, seem, suggest, tend
Adverbs: generally, possibly, relatively, seemingly, **usually**
Adjectives: probable, possible, **apparent**
Modal verbs: can, could, might
Modal nouns: likelihood, possibility, **tendency**

Note: The words in bold are extra examples that do not appear in our texts.

Task 3.3

This article endeavors to make some progress in those directions. It *shows* that both property- and knowledge-based resources that are hard to buy or imitate contributed to performance returns on sales, operating profits, and market share. However, the environmental context *was* all-important in conditioning these relationships. Periods of stability and predictability *favored* firms with property-based resources but did not reward those with knowledge-based resources. Precisely the opposite *was* true for periods of uncertainty, even though the sample of firms was identical. It follows, then that whether or not an asset can be considered a resource *will depend* as much on context enveloping an organization as on the properties of the asset itself. It *is* misleading to attempt to define resources independent of the tasks they are to serve and the environment within which they must function (cf. Barney, 1991).	indicates appears to have been apparently favored seems to have been is likely to depend appears to be

Task 3.4

1. The study did not include a cross-cultural comparison; therefore it is difficult to compare the results from previous studies (in the US) with the present German study.

2. The study was limited to mathematics; therefore, the results may not be generalisable to other homework subjects.

3. Data collection was restricted to 7th grade students; therefore, the generalisability of results to other grades may be affected.

4. The variable 'homework monitoring' was poorly defined. The study did not differentiate between merely checking that homework had been completed and actually marking and providing feedback on the homework, whereas previous studies were based on homework that was actually corrected. This is likely to limit the comparability of the studies.

5. The study was limited to variables that can be influenced by teachers, even though other variables may affect student performance. It is, therefore, not possible to be certain that achievement is not partly due to students performing related leisure-time activities.

6. Only academic outcomes were considered, even though there may also have been positive and/or negative nonacademic outcomes.

7. The research was not experimental; experimental trials may have produced clearer results.

Task 3.5

Hedges have been italicised.

Text 1: Discussion

Our results *suggested* that culvert attributes influence species' use but different attributes *appeared* to affect use by different species. One common theme at all scales of resolution — individual species, species group and community level — was that traffic volume, and to a lesser degree, noise levels and road width, ranked high as significant factors affecting species' use of culverts.

One would expect that as road width increased medium-sized forest mammals would be increasingly vulnerable. The risk of predation while attempting to cross exposed road corridors *may* be greater as well (Korpimaki & Norrdahl 1989; Rodriguez, Crema & Delibes 1996). Coyotes, being the largest of the mammal species studied, *tended* to use culverts less in high traffic density situations, whereas three of the four smaller mammals (martens, snowshoe hares and red squirrels), and not surprisingly the three-species group, showed greater use of the passages. Forrest-associated mammal species *generally* avoid open areas without overstorey or shrub cover (Buskirk & Powell 1994; Ruggiero et al. 1994) and we would expect the same response to an open corridor (Oxley, Fenton & Carmody 1974; Mader 1984; Swihart & Slade 1984). Culvert use by these species *might* be a response to this fragmented and unsafe habitat and a result of learned behaviour passed on by surviving individuals selecting culverts for cross-highway travel.

Text 2: Limitations of the Study

The findings of this study *are confined to physical abuse. Although the detrimental effect of mental abuse on a relationship should not be ignored,** only a small proportion of the women involved in this study complained of verbal or mental abuse. *The possibility* that mental abuse, by lowering the women's self-esteem, *may exacerbate* the effects of the physical abuse cannot be rejected, but a separate study would be needed to ratify such a suggestion.

A further note of caution is necessary when generalizing from this sample. The vast majority of the women studied came from low income families where the husband had relatively little education and the results, therefore, *may be* a function of the sample. Other studies, however, *have suggested* that neither of these variables increases *the possibility* of violence in a relationship; similar patterns of violence have been found in homes across the social spectrum and at all educational levels.

Perhaps the major limitation of this study is the sample size. However, the consistency of the pattern of the development of violence *suggests* that the observations would hold true for a larger sample.

* The 'although' clause here is acknowledging the importance of a factor that was not considered in the research to stress that the researchers are aware of the significance of this limitation. Compare with the use of 'although' clauses to soften criticism in Example 2.37 and Chapter 4: Subordination.

Text 3: Review of Literature/Discussion

As this brief walking tour through literary history *indicates,* <u>The Changing Light</u> draws equally from all kinds of literary tradition. The epic is promiscuous in the choice of its sources: like Seneca's bee, Merrill gathers the nectar of multiple poetic models and transforms it into the pure honey of his own magnum opus. Through his synthesis of autobiography and memory, through his free, indiscriminate, and *seemingly* haphazard borrowing from former literary works, the poet produces a controlled fantasy of becoming an equal with Homer, Dante, Spenser, Milton, Blake and Yeats. But putting Merrill in that notable company of literary masters only does injustice to his poetry as a whole; his remarks at Harvard were no doubt heartfelt, but also delicately sarcastic. Should we instead begin by trying to situate the trilogy in the tradition of the American long poem? <u>The Waste Land</u> *seems* a *likely* precursor, though *we can only go so far* in claiming Merrill's poetic affinity with Eliot. After the publication of the whole of <u>Sandover</u> in 1982, Merrill was promoted from customary inclusion in poetic anthologies to what at this point *seems* to be a permanent place in the history of twentieth-century American literature. In <u>The Western Canon</u> which came out more than a decade after <u>Sandover</u>, Harold Bloom regards Merrill as *probably* the most important American poet of the latter part of the twentieth century next to John Ashbery.

Chapter 4

Task 4.1

Summary of the research: Sentences 1–3
Contribution: Sentences 4–16
Limitations: Sentence 17
Further research: Sentences 18 & 19

Task 4.2

Text 1

Limitations:	Sentences 1, 3
Further research:	Sentences 2, 4, 8, final part of 11
Contribution:	Sentences 5–7,* 10
Summary of research:	Sentences 9, first part of 11

* Sentences 5 and 6 do not actually point to the contribution, but explain the shortcomings of the traditional procedures, which this new procedure could replace. These sentences are needed to give meaning to Sentence 7.

Text 2

Summary of the research:	Sentences 1–4
Implications:	Sentences 5–8
Limitations:	Sentence 9 (phrase 'if also necessarily provisional')
Contribution:	Sentence 9

Text 3

It is difficult to clearly separate the elements in this conclusion. All the sentences seem to be summarising what has been discovered and simultaneously making recommendations to concerned parties. The contribution is implied throughout the passage as the recommendations appear to be offering a new approach to practitioners in the field.

This combining of functions within a sentence is fairly common in journal articles where there is a requirement for brevity imposed by word limitations. However, if recommendations form a major component of a dissertation outcome, they are generally clearly separated from other elements in the concluding section/chapter.

Task 4.3

Text 1

1(a) highlights the controversial use of the ISO 9000 standard, whereas 1(b) gives prominence to the fact that the use of ISO 9000 standard provides a definite and practical way to establish a management system. A researcher wishing to support the use of ISO 9000 would choose to write 1(b).

Text 2

2(a) focuses on the advantages of urine tests, while 2(b) pinpoints the fact that urine tests are less sensitive for diagnostic purposes. A researcher promoting the use of urine tests would choose to write 2(a).

Task 4.4

1. The purpose is to study recidivism among boot camp completers. (Sentence 3, first part)
2. The research was carried out because recidivism is a problem (**this is implied, not explicitly stated, in Sentence 1**), and recidivism reduction is an important objective of boot camps. (Sentences 1–2)
3. Recidivism is studied among boot camp completers in eight stages of community supervision using two or more recidivism measures and making cross-group comparisons across states (**this research was conducted in the US**). (Sentences 3 (second part), 5)
4. The researcher discovered that there was not necessarily a difference in recidivism between those who had completed boot camps and their counterparts. (Sentence 6)
5. The researcher comes to the **conclusion** that the effectiveness of boot camps varies from state to state, and that the programme itself cannot, therefore, be judged as successful or otherwise. (Sentence 7)

Task 4.5

It is possible to remove certain words/phrases from Version A for several reasons:
1. information unnecessary to the understanding of the text:
   in Europe, friend, Charles Louis, lengthy
2. information unnecessary because it is obvious from the context:
   relating to several of Adam's architectural interiors, any of, first

3. phrases unnecessary because a briefer construction says the same thing:
    has long been, who was, in light of these findings, it seems that, roles ... in influencing

Task 4.6

One possible way of reducing this abstract is as follows:

> The Home Mortgage Disclosure Act (HMDA) mandates the reporting of mortgage loan applications. [1] Most recent studies of mortgage lending patterns rely on HMDA data, even though some mortgages go unreported. [2] Understanding the relationship between HMDA coverage and neighborhood characteristics is important because neighborhood application rates and HMDA loan originations are used to measure neighborhood lending activity. [3] If HMDA coverage rates vary systematically with neighborhood characteristics, studies that use these characteristics yield biased results. [4]
>
> This paper estimates the fraction of mortgage activity reported under HMDA, and examines how HMDA coverage rates vary with neighborhood racial and income characteristics. [5] Independent (non-HMDA) loans purchased were compared with loans reported as sold in HMDA datasets in the two years before and after HMDA. [6] The major finding is that the 1993 HMDA dataset contains only around 75% of the total mortgage loans, an improvement of only 5% from 1992, despite the increased reporting requirements for 1993. [7] The HMDA files for both years exhibit substantial variability in coverage across census tracts and lenders, but the direction of bias is consistent. [8] Measured HMDA coverage rates are higher in lower income census tracts, relative to higher income tracts. [9] [190 words]

Task 4.7

Answers will depend on student's choice of articles.

Chapter 5

Task 5.1

Answer will depend on student's own research.

Task 5.2

1. Yes, very informative.
2. No, much too broad. We need to know what kind of impact is being considered, what sort of environmental measures are being used. The final title submitted was:

   The negative impact of environmental pollution control measures on the industrial and manufacturing areas of Singapore.
3. Yes.
4. No, this is such a vast topic covering all levels of education that an in-depth study of the whole of it could not be done within the time allowed for a postgraduate degree. The title has to show the delimitations of the research in terms of levels, aspects, and possibly even regions to be covered.
5. Yes.

Task 5.3

1. Job discrimination and psychiatric disabilities/Discrimination in the workplace and psychiatric disabilities
2. Limitations of the Study

Task 5.4

1. The main chapter headings are in italics. This is not appropriate as italics usually indicate subordinated points.
2. The lack of indentation throughout makes the relationship between headings and subheadings difficult to comprehend.
3. The subheadings in points 4.1 and 4.2 are not at all helpful as readers do not know the research hypotheses.

4. 'Prologue' is not appropriate for the background information in an academic text.
5. It is not usual to have a separate chapter for research design and questions.

Suggestions for layout:

Task 5.5

Text 1

(a) The signposts are underlined in the text below.
(b) The signposts are explicit.
(c) The signposts are adequate in that they explain clearly how the paper is organised.

> The aim of this paper is to demonstrate the relevance of possible-world frameworks to the study of poetic text worlds. <u>My argument will proceed as follows</u>. <u>In the first part of the paper</u>, I will briefly discuss the development of the notion of possible worlds from logic to the semantics of fictionality, and consider the way in which a possible-world approach can be used to describe and classify fictional worlds; I will focus particularly on the framework developed by Ryan (1991a, 1991b). <u>In the second part of the paper</u>, I will show how possible-world models, and specifically Ryan's approach, can be applied to poetry. In particular, I will adopt a possible-world perspective in order to consider:
> i.   the internal structure of the world projected by a particular poem;
> ii. the projection of deviant situations of address;
> iii. the description of different types of poetic worlds.
> <u>I will conclude</u> with a discussion of the main weaknesses of possible-world frameworks, and with some suggestions for future developments in the study of text worlds.

Text 2

(a) The signposts are underlined in the text below.
(b) The signposts are explicit.
(c) Some people might find these signposts confusing, particularly the use of 'the following section' twice and the use of 'next' after 'the following'. In a situation like this, where there are many sections, it may be clearer to use numerals (the first section, the second section etc.) to signal the organisation.

> The <u>next section of this paper</u> describes the housing policy situation in a number of Latin American countries, including Bolivia, to provide some comparative contexts for the FONVIS program. <u>The following section</u> details the low-income urban housing situation in Bolivia with emphasis on the largest cities,

i.e. La Paz, El Alto, and Santa Cruz (figure 1). <u>Next</u>, the FONVIS program and its achievements up to and including 1994 are described, while <u>the following section</u> outlines the shortcomings of the organization's approach. <u>Finally, the paper concludes</u> with specific recommendations regarding how the FONVIS program might be modified to actually address the needs of those without access to housing credit.

Text 3

(a) The signposts are underlined in the text below.

(b) This text uses both explicit and implicit signposts. We can deduce that the empirical section follows the hypotheses, although this is not explicitly stated. We can also assume the secondary comparison follows the main comparison of job satisfaction and stress levels of GPs on salaried contracts and those on standard GMS contracts.

(c) The signposts are adequate in that they indicate the organisation of the paper up to the conclusion, but a final indication of what the 'end' of the paper includes would have been helpful.

This paper explores the association between type of contract and job satisfaction and stress levels by studying the introduction of salaried contracts in the UK. <u>In the first section</u> we develop simple hypotheses to be tested using descriptive information on salaried contracts in PMS pilots. <u>In the empirical section</u> we use data from two surveys to compare job satisfaction and stress levels of GPs on salaried contracts with GPs on the standard GMS contract. A secondary comparison is made to establish whether job satisfaction is higher in PMS pilot sites more generally by comparing GPs on salaried contract with their PMS GP employers (referred to as non-salaried PMS GPs).

Task 5.6

1. Three aspects of life that affect the theory and model of African American drug use.
2. The differences between first contact and long-term patients in perceived QoL.

Task 5.7

Text 1

Sentence	Noun/noun phrase	Verb
1	The findings of the study	support (active)
	the percentage of minority students	is*
2	Data in table 5	show (active)

This extract is from the discussion.

Text 2

Sentence	Noun/noun phrase	Verb
1	The argument	has*
2	The first ('part' is elided)	is*
3	It (replacing 'the first part')	suggests (active)
		does (active)
4	The second ('part' is elided)	examines (active)
5	It (replacing 'the second part')	aims (active)
6	The final section	reassesses (active)

* These verbs have no passive form.

This extract is from the end of the introduction.

Chapter 6

Task 6.1

Sentence	Given information	Referring back to	Sentence
2	Under the new environment	environment ... has changed	(1)
3	Such a change	environment ... has changed	(1)
4	The first process	three parallel processes	(3)
5	The second process	three parallel processes	(3)
7	One way	two major ways	(6)
8	The other way	two major ways	(6)
9	As a consequence of such restructuring	industrial restructuring	(6)
10	The new institutional structure	institutional structure	(8)
11	In between the central government and enterprises, local governments	ministries, provincial governments and enterprises	(8)

Note:

Sentence 6 does not follow the given-new pattern because it begins with a term that has not been mentioned before '*Industrial restructuring*'. This is acceptable occasionally, particularly when the term is immediately equated with given information; it is only when many sentences in a paragraph begin with a new (i.e. previously unmentioned) term that the writing becomes difficult to follow.

Task 6.2

Answers will depend on student's choice of text.

Task 6.3

The following is one way to rewrite this piece of writing to reduce the number of connectors.

Traffic congestion is most serious in Hong Kong during rush hours, around 7.00 to 9.00 in the morning and 5.00 to 7.30 in the afternoon. There are significant spatial variations, but a number of black spots exist where congestion during peak hours is especially bad. These include the entrance of the Cross Harbour Tunnel, Central district and the Tsing Yi Bridge, as well as Caine Road, where the road, like many in Hong Kong, is very narrow.

A recent increase in dependence on public transport, such as on buses, trains and subways has affected traffic flow. This increase, however, has not been spread evenly, with about 80% of the total demand for public transport being confined to a mere 20 hours of the week. During rush hours all the public transport facilities are fully utilized. At other times public transport suffers from the problem of too few passengers, resulting in bus companies cutting the number of buses to reduce their operating costs. This leads to inconvenience for the public, who have to wait longer for their bus.

The lack of parking spaces creates a further problem in Hong Kong. With the high density of buildings and narrow streets, there are very few possible places to park. Consequently, even with low levels of car ownership, the streets and often the footpaths are choked with parked vehicles. For example, many cars are parked along Garden Road in Central District, which is narrow and steep, so drivers have to be very careful when negotiating the sharp, very dangerous corner.

Task 6.4

1. *The words used by psychologists are a constant source of anxiety to them. **They** also cause rage to their readers (including other psychologists). If **they** coin a new term, they may be accused of creating ugly and unnecessary neologisms.*

The first 'They' is fine, as it clearly refers to 'The words'. However, 'they' at the beginning of the third sentence would then also have to refer to 'The words' and this is obviously not possible. Clarity would be best achieved by using the noun 'psychologists' at the beginning of Sentence 3.

2. *If the open-area is larger than 3, filtration efficiency reaches a plateau, or* ***it*** *declines as* ***it*** *gets smaller.*

   Again the first 'it' is clear; it refers to 'filtration efficiency'. We would assume in this case that the second 'it' has the same reference, but that is not possible. As in Sentence 1, we need to use a noun: 'the open-area'.

3. *The proposal is to build a small shopping centre with specialised goods to sell.* ***It*** *doesn't imply that only one item is sold, but that the shops focus on a particular group of customers.*

   If 'It' at the beginning of the second sentence was correct, it would have to refer to 'The proposal', but, in fact, it refers to 'the concept of building a small shopping centre with specialised goods to sell'. Therefore, 'It' should be replaced by 'This' or 'This concept'. 'It' has to refer to an identifiable singular, countable noun or an uncountable noun in the previous text, not to the whole idea or the whole sentence.

4. *The Public Utilities Regulatory Policy Act (PURPA) required regulated electric utilities to buy electricity from independent cogenerators at the 'avoided cost' of having to construct additional capacity.* ***This*** *spawned the independent power production (IPP) market in the United States.*

   The use of 'This' is correct, as it refers to the idea presented in the previous sentence, i.e. the requirement introduced by the Act, not to the Act itself.

5. *COD removal efficiency in the second stage was little higher than that in the first stage.* ***It*** *was mainly due to the higher influent COD concentration.*

   'It' should be replaced by 'This' as the reference is to the result reported in the previous sentence, not to 'COD removal efficiency'.

6. *The government seems to be on the point of collapse.* **It** *is because several scandals involving leading figures have surfaced in recent weeks.*

    'It' should be replaced by 'This' as the reference is to the government being on the point of collapse, not to 'the government'. It would also be possible and, in fact, more usual, to make one sentence of these two by omitting 'This is' so that the reason and result are presented together.

7. *I am particularly interested in examining the reasons why people speak differently in different social contexts, how the social functions of language are realised and how language is used to convey meaning.* **These** *will enable me to develop a deeper understanding of the problems that students face when learning a new language.*

    'These' at the beginning of the second sentence is not referring to the factors that will be studied, but to the examination of those factors that will be carried out by the writer; therefore, 'These' should be replaced by 'This' or 'This examination'.

Task 6.5

Here is one possible way of splitting the sentence in two:

> Such an approach integrates theory and research into the nature of language learning and use, with insights derived from the observation and analysis of what actually goes on in classrooms (as opposed to what some say should go on). It uses this knowledge to inform the issues raised and points made.

Sources

The following indicate the sources for examples and tasks. Where the texts are above 250 words, permission has been granted.

Chapter 1

Example/ Task	Pages	Source
Example 1.1	9–10	Qianru Zhu, Wenju Jia, F.H.White & Xianliang Chang. (1994). DNA Ploidy and Proliferate Pattern in Benign Pleomorphic Adenomas of Major Salivary Glands. University of Hong Kong.
Task 1.1	11–13	Semino, Elena. (1996) Possible Worlds in Poetry. *Journal of Literary Semantics*. Vol. 25/3: 189–224. Reproduced with permission from Mouton De Gruyter.
Task 1.2 Texts 1 & 2	21–22	Adapted from materials developed by David Nunan.
Examples 1.4 & 1.5	26–27	Sanderson, P. (2001). Age and Gender Issues in Adolescent Attitudes to Dance. *European Physical Education Review* 7/2: 117–36.
Example 1.8	27	Salunkhe, D. K., Chavan, J. K. & Kadam, S. S. (1990). *Dietary Tannins: Consequences and Remedies*. Florida: CRC Press.
Example 1.9	28	Pels, E., Nijkamp, P. & Reitveld, P. (2001). Airport and Airline Choice in a Multiple Airport Region: An Empirical Analysis for the San Francisco Bay Area. *Regional Studies* 35/1: 1–9.
Task 1.4: Text 1	29	McManus, A. M., Armstrong, N. & Williams, C. A. (1997). Effect of Training on the Aerobic Power and Anaerobic Performance of Prepubertal Girls. *Acta Paediatr* 86: 456–9.

Chapter 2

Example/ Task	Pages	Source
Task 2.1: All extracts	42–43	Jordan, F. M., Murdoch, B. E., Buttsworth, D.L. & Hudson-Tennent, J. (1994). Speech and Language Performance of Brain-injured Children. *Aphasiology* 9: 23–32. Reprinted by permission of Psychology Press Ltd.
Task 2.2: Extracts 1 & 2	48–49	Hasell, M. J., Peatross, F. D. & Bono, C (1993). Gender Choice and Domestic Space: Preferences for Kitchens in Married Households. *Journal of Architectural and Planning Research* 10/1: 1–22. Reproduced with permission of the *Journal of Architectural and Planning Research* published by Locke Science Publishing Co. Inc.
Example 2.22	50	Salager-Meyer, Francoise. (1994). Hedges and Textual Communicative Function in Medical English Written Discourse. *English for Specific Purposes* 13/2: 149–70.
Examples 2.24 & 2.25	51	Miltenburg, D. M., Conklin, L. & Saskri, S. (2000). The Role of Genetic Screening and Prophylactic Surgery in Surgical Oncology. *Journal of American College of Surgeons* 190/5: 605–14.
Examples 2.26 & 2.29	52, 55	Layton Mackenzie, D., Brame, R., McDowall, D. & Souryal, C. (1995). Boot Camp Prisons and Recidivism in Eight States. *Criminology* 33/3: 327–55.
Example 2.32	56	Dong, Y. R. (1996). Learning How to Use Citations for Knowledge Transformations: Non-Native Doctoral Students' Dissertation Writing in Science. *Research in the Teaching of English* 30: 428–40.
Example 2.33 & Task 2.4: Text 2	57, 59–60	Oldham, G. & Cummings, A.(1996). Employee Creativity: Personal and Contextual Factors at Work. *Academy of Management Journal* Vol.39/3: 607–34.
Task 2.4: Text 1	58–59	Leiger-Vargus, K., Mandorff-Shrestha, S. A., Featherstone, J. B. D. & Gwinner, L. M. (1995). Effects of Sodium Bicarbonate Dentifrices on the Level of Cariogenic Bacteria in Human Saliva. *Journal of the European Organisation of Caries Research*: 143–7.
Task 2.5	62–63	Lee, Dae Hyun (1996). Clinical and Microbiological Effects of Metronidazole Dental Gel in Treated Adult Periodontitis Subjects. Unpublished MDS dissertation, The University of Hong Kong.

Chapter 3

Example/ Task	Pages	Source
Task 3.1	70–71	Harrison, S., MacLennan, R., Speare, R. & Wronski, L. (1994). Sun Exposure and Melanocytic Naevi in Young Australian Children. *Lancet* 334: 1529–32.
Examples 3.1 & 3.6	72, 75	Yi'an, W. (1998). What Do Tests of Listening Comprehension Test? A Retrospective Study of EFL Test-takers Performing a Multiple-choice Task. *Language Testing* 15/1: 28.
Examples 3.2 & 3.7	72, 75	Venugopalan H. S., Mohney, S. E., DeLucca, J. M. & Molnar, R. J. (1999). Approaches to Designing Thermally Stable Schottky Contacts to n-GaN. *Semicond, Sci. Technology.* 14: 757–61.
Example 3.3	72	Crain, M. (2001). Control Beliefs of the Frail Elderly. *Care Management Journals* 3/1: 42–5.
Example 3.4	73	Sanger, J., Komorowski, R., Larson, D., Gingrass, R., Yousif, N., Matloub, H. (1995) Tissue Humoral Response to Intact and Ruptured Silicone Gel-Filled Prostheses. *Plastic and Reconstructive Surgery.* Vol. 95. May 6: 1033–37.
Example 3.12	79–80	Killingray, D. (2001) African Voices from Two World Wars. *Historical Research.* 74/186: 425–43.
Example 3.14	83–84	Chen, Tong (1995). *Application of UASB Technology in Treating Wastewater Containing Aromatic Compounds.* Unpublished MPhil thesis, The University of Hong Kong.
Example 3.16	85	Hong, Jiang (2001). The Masculine-Feminine Woman: Transcending Gender Identity in Zhang Xinxin's Fiction. *China Information* XV/1: 138–65.
Task 3.3	85–86	Miller, D. & Shamsie, J. (1996). The Resource-based View of the Firm in Two Environments: The Hollywood Film Studios 1936–1965. *Academy Management Journal* 39/3: 519–43.
Example 3.17	86–87	Ranney, M. & Aranda, M. (2001). Factors Associated with Depressive Symptoms among Latino Family Dementia Caregivers. *Journal of Ethnic and Cultural Diversity in Social Work* 10/1: 1–21.

(continued on p. 196)

Example/ Task	Pages	Source
Task 3.4	88–90	Trautwein, U., Koller, O., Schmitz, B. & Baumert, J. (2001). Do Homework Assignments Enhance Achievement? A Multilevel Analysis in 7th Grade Mathematics. *Contemporary Educational Psychology* 27: 26–50. Reprinted by permission from Elsevier.
Task 3.5: Text 1	91	Clevenger, A. P., Chruszcz, B. & Gunson, K. (2001). Drainage Culverts as Habitat Linkages and Factors Affecting Passage by Mammals. *Journal of Applied Ecology* 38: 1340–9 (p. 1346).
Task 3.5: Text 2	91–92	Bugental, D. B. & Shennum, W. (2002). Gender, Power and Violence in the Family. *Child Management* 7/1: 56–64.
Task 3.5: Text 3	92	Gwiazda, P. (2001). Views from the Rosebrick Manor: Poetic Authority in James Merrill's *The Changing Light at Sandover*. *Texas Studies in Literature and Language* 34/4: 418–31.

Chapter 4

Example/ Task	Pages	Source
Example 4.1	97–98	Guttery, R. S. (2002). The Effects of Subdivision Design on Housing Values: The Case of Alleyways. *Journal of Real Estate Research* 23/3: 265–73. Reprinted by permission from the *Journal of Real Estate Research*.
Example 4.2	98–99	Foster, P. & Skehan, P. (1999). Influence of Source of Planning and Focus of Planning. *Language Teaching Research* 3/3: 215–45. Reprinted by permission from Arnold Publishers.
Example 4.3	100	Fraser, C. J. (1999). *Similarity and Standards: Language, Cognition and Action in Chinese and Western Thought*. Unpublished PhD dissertation, The University of Hong Kong.
Example 4.4	103	Slentz, C. S., Torgan, C. E., Houmard, J. A., Tanner, C. & Kraus, W. E (2002). Long-term Effects of Exercise Training and Detraining on Carbohydrate Metabolism in Overweight Subjects. *Clinical Exercise Physiology* 4/1: 22–8.

(continued on p. 197)

Example/ Task	Pages	Source
Example 4.5	104–105	Getzner, M. (2002). Investigating Public Decisions about Protecting Wetlands. *Journal of Environmental Management* 64, 237–46. Reprinted by permission from Elsevier.
Example 4.6	105–106	Martyn, E. (2002). *The Effects of Task Type on Negotiation of Meaning in Small Group Work.* Unpublished PhD dissertation, The University of Hong Kong.
Task 4.2: Text 1; Task 4.3: Text 2	106–107, 111	Wong, K. C., Ho, B. S. W., Egglestone, S. I. and Lewis, W. H. (1994). Diagnosis of Urogenital Gonorrhoea: Evaluation of an Enzyme Immunoassay and Use of Urine as a Non-invasive Specimen. *British Journal of Biomedical Science* 51: 312–5. Reprinted by permission of Institute of Biomedical Science.
Task 4.2: Text 2	107–108	Richardson, B. (1997). Remapping the Present: The Master Narrative of Modern Literary History and the Lost Forms of Twentieth Century Fiction. *20th Century Literature* 43: 201–305.
Task 4.2: Text 3	108	Tully, B. (2002). The Evaluations of Reactions in Sexual Abuse Cases. *Child Abuse Review* 11: 94–102.
Example 4.10	110–111	Oldham, G. & Cummings, A. (1996). Employee Creativity: Personal and Contextual Factors at Work. *Academy of Management Journal* 29/3: 607–34.
Example 4.11	113	Holmes, A. & James, J. (1996). Discrimination, Lending Practices and Housing Values: Preliminary Evidence from the Houston Market. *The Journal of Real Estate and Research* 11/1: 25–34.
Example 4.12	114–115	Li Ping-ying, Eria (1998). Self-determination of Young Adults with Mental Handicap: Implications for Education and Vocational Preparation. Unpublished PhD dissertation, The University of Hong Kong.
Task 4.4	116	Layton Mackenzie, D., Brame, R., McDowell, D. & Souryal, C. (1995). Boot Camp Prisons and Recidivism in Eight States. *Criminology* 33/3: 327–55.
Task 4.6	118–119	Berkovec, J. & Zorn, P. (1996). How Complete is HMDA? HMDA Coverage of Freddie Mac Purchases. *Journal of Real Estate Research* 11/1: 39–49. Reprinted by permission of the *Journal of Real Estate Research*.
Example 4.15	122	Swanson, N. G., Galinsky, T. L., Cole, L. L., Pan, C. S. & Sauter, S. L. (1997). The Impact of Keyboard Design on Comfort and Productivity in a Text-Entry Task. *Applied Ergonomics* 28/1: 9–16.

Chapter 5

Example/ Task	Pages	Source
Task 5.3: Extract 1	136	Pardeck, J. T. (1999). Psychiatric Disabilities and the Americans with Disabilities Act: Implications for Policy and Practice. *Journal of Health and Social Policy*, 10/3: 2.
Task 5.3: Extract 2	136	Chi, I. and Leung, E. M. F. (1999). Health Promotion for Elderly Persons in Hong Kong. *Journal of Health and Social Policy* 10/3: 48.
Examples 5.6 & 5.7	137	Li, Kam Cheong (1999). Linguistic Consciousness and Writing Performance. Unpublished PhD dissertation, The University of Hong Kong.
Example 5.9	140	Messick, S. (1994). Alternative Modes of Assessment, Uniform Standards of Validity. Paper presented at 'Evaluating Alternatives to Traditional Testing for Selection' Conference, sponsored by Bowling Green State University, 25–26 October 1994.
Example 5.10	140	Berger, P. (1963). *Invitation to Sociology*. London: Penguin Books.
Example 5.11	140–141	Gallimore, P. (1996). Confirmation Bias in the Valuation Process: A Test for Corroborating Evidence. *Journal of Property Research* 13: 261–73.
Example 5.12	141–142	Martyn, E. (2002). The Effects of Task Type on Negotiation of Meaning in Small Group Work. Unpublished PhD dissertation, The University of Hong Kong.
Example 5.13	142	Fay, S. J. (1993). The Rise and Fall of Tagging as a Criminal Justice Measure in Britain. *International Journal of the Sociology of Law* 21/3: 307–18.
Task 5.5: Extract 1	143	Semino, E. (1996) Possible Worlds in Poetry. *Journal of Literary Semantics* XXV/3: 190. Reproduced with permission of Mouton De Gruyter.
Task 5.5: Extract 2 & Example 5.15	143–144, 146	Daniere, A. G. (1999). More and Better Credit: Housing Policy Reform in Bolivia. *International Planning Studies* 4/1: 30.
Task 5.5: Extract 3	144	Gosden, T., Williams, J., Petchy, R., Leese, B. & Sibbald, B. (2002) Salaried Contracts in UK General Practice: A Study of Job Satisfaction and Stress. *Journal of Health Services* 7: 26–33.

(continued on p. 199)

Example/ Task	Pages	Source
Task 5.6: Extract 1	145	Brunswick, A. F. (1999). Structural Strain: An Ecological Paradigm for Studying African American Drug Use. *Drugs and Society* 14/1–2: 7.
Task 5.6: Extract 2	145	Lang, A., Steiner, E., Berghofer, G., Henkel, H., Schmitz, M., Schmidl, F. & Rudas, S. (2002). Quality of Life and Other Characteristics of Viennese Mental Health Users. *International Journal of Social Psychiatry* 48/1: 59–69 (p. 67).
Task 5.7: Extract 1	147	Mikitovics, A. & Crehan, K. (2002). Pre-professional Skills Test Scores as College of Education Admission Criteria. *Educational Research* 95/4: 215–22.
Task 5.7: Extract 2	147–148	Thompson, J. (1998). The Genesis of the 1906 Trade Union Disputes Act: Liberalism, Trade Unions, and the Law. *Twentieth Century British History* 9/2: 175–200.

Chapter 6

Example/ Task	Pages	Source
Statements/ Version B	154–155	Nunan, D. (1990). *Language Teaching Methodology*. London: Prentice Hall.
Task 6.1 & Example 6.2	156–157, 161	Wang, J. J. and Liu W. (1998). The Dynamic Relationship between Central Government and Local Authorities in Orienting Foreign Direct Investment: A case study of the automotive industry. In Lee, S. M. and Tang, W. S. (eds.) *The Spatial Economic Development in Mainland China*. Hong Kong: Chinese University Press.
Example 6.1	157–158	McKenna, J. J. I. (1986). A Qualitative and Quantitative Analysis of the Anterior Dentition Visible in Photographs and its Application to Forensic Odontology. Unpublished MPhil thesis, The University of Hong Kong.

Index